Praise for *Trove*

"For so many of us, the obsessions of our future selves are sown into the wounds of our past. This is so clearly the case with Sandra Miller, an immensely gifted memoirist for whom the search for treasure has been, among other things, a lifelong search for beauty, for safety, for the revealing of secrets that may become a sanctuary for love. The prose here is spare yet lyrical, evocative and painstakingly honest, and *Trove*, itself, is a treasure."

—ANDRE DUBUS III, *New York Times* bestselling author
of *House of Sand and Fog*

"Sandra Miller's memoir, *Trove,* grabs readers by the heartstrings and whisks us along on her life's journey. From New York to California to Japan, from Europe to Boston, Miller's story is a marvelous, sometimes magical adventure that is also urgent, heartbreaking. Miller is eloquent, witty, and grippingly honest as she searches for love and treasure, within and wi   *Trove* is that rare treasure of a book—a compelling st   ˜hes your heart and soul."

—MAUREEN STANTON, auth   .ckward:
                                                  t Girlhood

"Sandra Miller's writing is s   magick. Going beyond words, she makes yo   vriting moves you to explore and ponder, and best   s up the imagination to all things possible."

—DAMIEN ECHOLS, author of *High Magick* and the
New York Times bestseller *Life After Death*

"You will not read a page of this book without thinking, *oh my God, I have so been there*. Sandra Miller's *Trove* is a hilarious, heartbreaking page-turner about one woman's relentless search for the treasures life has to offer: romantic love, parental approval, a decent career, and some shred of meaning in this crazy world. *Trove* is the utterly accessible memoir we've all been hungering for: the everywoman's *Eat Pray Love*."

—ERICA FERENCIK, author of *Into the Jungle*

"With dazzling prose, keen observation, and laugh-out-loud humor, *Trove* is an essential book for women braving middle age, or anyone looking back in life before they surge forward. Sandra Miller writes about marriage, parenting, aging parents, and the quest for creative fulfillment with wisdom and insight, and with an honesty that is as shocking as it is satisfying."

—LISA CAREY, author of *The Stolen Child*

TROVE

A WOMAN'S SEARCH *for* TRUTH *and* BURIED TREASURE

SANDRA A. MILLER

Brown Paper Press
Long Beach, CA

Brown Paper Press
6475 E. Pacific Coast Highway, #329
Long Beach, CA 90803

Library of Congress Control Number: 2019938729

ISBN: 978-1-94193-212-4
978-1-94193-214-8 (ebook)

FIRST EDITION

Cover Design by Joan Wong
Interior Design by Gary Rosenberg

14 13 12 11 10 / 10 9 8 7 6 5 4 3 2 1

This is the moment of embarking.
All auspicious signs are in place.

—DENG MING-DAO

Prologue

At five years old I began hunting for treasure. I looked for it on sidewalks, under trees, in the dressing room at Sears where pockets released loose coins, matchbooks, ticket stubs, and foil gum wrapper linings that held their shape like a magic trick. I found the dirty penny kicked beneath the counter at Liggett's Drug Store, and the twisted piece of telephone wire that called to me from the gutter. Walking home from church, I filled my black patent leather purse with discarded fragments from my Connecticut factory town, as if they were clues leading me to even bigger treasure that lay far from my home, a stifling white colonial that could not contain my wants.

When forced inside I looked out. Standing in front of the sliding glass door of our dining room, I imagined treasures buried beneath the front lawn where a birdfeeder hung from the lowest branch of the dogwood tree. Behind me, my tall, ruddy father, sloe-eyed handsome like an old movie star, sat bent over his newspaper, while my mother, brittle-thin and blonde, circled him in her ritual dance of rage. Around the dining room table she went, picking up a silver-plated candlestick then pounding it back down, stomping her feet dramatically, brandishing her arms with a huff.

My father yelled, "What the hell, Betty?"

She yelled back, "I'll give you 'What the hell'!"

He slammed down his fist so hard that the plate split in two, the meat landing on one half, the baked potato on the other, as if even the food was taking sides. My mother retreated to find a cigarette, shutting her eyes on that first deep drag. "A cigarette?" my father scoffed. "That's how you deal with things?"

"Says the guy who smashed a plate," she bit back.

When I screamed for them to stop, please stop, he stood, this gruff giant, and walloped me across the back, while my older sister, Betsy, cowered in the corner of our dining room with its dull ivory wallpaper. A week could go by without my parents exchanging a word. They just shuffled around each other in chilling rebuff.

One February morning, staring out at our birdfeeder and dead winter lawn, I wished myself away from them forever.

What happened next was both simple and profound. A large crow, feathers as black and glossy as midnight, alit on the feeder's platform. My mother always banged her palm on the window to shoo the crows away—"greedy birds," she called them—but not me. This crow had intense eyes perfect for spotting sparkly bits of treasure, and a long beak that could carry it away. We were looking for the same things; I felt it in my chest—an invisible string connecting the crow's marble-sized heart to mine. It was such a muscular tug that when she tipped her head and dove at the ground, my own mouth opened in want, like a baby rooting for her mother's breast. In the next instant, she lifted her head and turned her jewel eyes to mine. In her beak was a shiny white stone. A gem I had missed.

I held myself still, afraid of snapping the thread that bound me to this vigilant bird. I dug my toes into the beige carpet, dry against my bare feet, and felt the cold on my face, as the winter air breached the wall of glass. When I tented my fingers against the window, the crow sensed the vibration and, in one fluid movement, spread her wings, folded back her feet, and disappeared into the high branches of the maple tree shadowing our yard. And some shiny part of me went with her, the thread pulling wisps through the window, the way a kite catches flight on a gust of wind.

I already had learned how not to cry because crying would be punished. Still, I wanted to weep at that goodbye. When someone says she feels her heart being ripped away, I understand. I do. I remember that moment, my cheek pressed against the glass, my mouth creating a cloud of breath as I strained to see where the crow had gone, teasing me with that small white stone and trailing behind her pieces of my heart.

1 - PUZZLED

"We should probably search together," my friend David suggested, "until we have a reason not to."

"Sounds good," I said, as quick to agree with him as I had been to argue with my husband, Mark, who wanted me to skip this excursion. I'm often nicer to men I'm not married to, something Mark just loves about me.

David and I began, wading side-by-side through an overgrown patch of spring weeds bordering the community garden in Brooklyn's Floyd Bennett Field. Sporting raggedy jeans and long-sleeved T-shirts, we could have passed as gardeners, only we weren't there to spread mulch or check on seedlings. We had no legitimate interest in the garden itself, but rather what we hoped lay beneath the cool May dirt: a pirate's treasure chest.

David had spent dozens of hours at home solving clues related to this armchair treasure hunt, a pastime in which a person or organization buries a prize and then sets up a series of puzzles to reveal the exact location. This hunt, called *We Lost Our Gold*, had been put in place by two enterprising puppeteers as a promotional stunt for their work; anyone with some free time and a computer could have a go at decoding the layers of complex clues concealed in eight YouTube videos about pirates struggling to recollect the whereabouts of their missing treasure. Once someone had correctly solved all of the clues, they would know precisely where in New York City to dig up the chest, which is what we were trying to do. David had determined that the garden in this defunct airport-turned-park was the X that marked the spot.

"What's actually *in* the treasure chest?" my husband of almost fifteen years asked when I presented my plan to spend a day digging in Brooklyn with a guy who wasn't him. Mark was sprawled on the couch reading *Golf Magazine* with one pair of glasses placed sexily atop the other.

"Ten thousand gold coins," I explained.

"Like doubloons?" he asked, incredulous.

"No, the golden dollar kind with Sacagawea and the presidents."

Mark, who with his shock of dark hair and full lips resembled both a young Warren Beatty and an ageless Mick Jagger, took off the top pair of glasses and set it on his stomach. "Ooh. I love that band," he said, "Sacagawea and the Presidents."

"Seriously."

"Seriously? There's a lot going on that day. The kids have stuff to get to. I'm working late. We have dinner plans."

"But there's always a lot going on."

"So are you telling me you're going or asking me if it works for you to go?"

"I'm telling you that I *want* to go." I crossed my arms over my chest, as if to suppress the ache I felt inside.

"And I'm telling you Friday is hard."

I drew a breath and tried to keep to the script: *Of course, it doesn't work for us. Of course, the kids come first. Of course, no sensible forty-six-year-old mother drives from Boston to Brooklyn to dig for treasure with a guy friend, while her husband handles work, house, kids, and meals.*

Here's what I refrained from saying: *My life depends upon this treasure hunt.*

But there are some things you simply can't explain, like the crow

that flew off with a piece of your heart and the chronic need to look for what you lost that day. Or the feeling that a treasure hunt could be the answer to a lifetime of longing. I just blew out of the house and headed for the bike path, my eyes blurred with tears for that part of myself I could never show: an insatiable craving for fullness.

Standing in front of the community garden with David, I listened attentively as he explained his deductive process, like the physicist that he is. "If you're going to bury a 160-pound wooden chest, there are a few key constraints," he said.

I pulled my small reporter's pad from my bag and started scribbling notes.

"For starters," he continued, "you would probably want to put the chest in public land within about one hundred yards of a parking lot. That way, whoever finds it could actually carry the thing out to their car."

"Of course!" I said, scrawling even faster, adding girly flourishes to my letters, stopping short of dotting my *i's* with puffy hearts in exhilaration over escaping with David for the entire day.

"And," he continued with casual confidence, "it should be in a place without much foot traffic, so someone won't just stumble on it or get arrested digging it up. I know if I were going to make a treasure hunt, I would bury it in a community garden."

"That," I said, poking my pen in the air between us, "is why you're so good at this."

He flashed me a questioning look. "What do you mean?"

David had dark, wavy hair and blue eyes that could focus like lasers. While I admitted to Mark that I always had a crush on him in that *yeah-he's-a-cute-dad* way, I never revealed the extent to which David stirred up unbidden longing, the kind that is systematically, if subliminally, prohibited by marriage vows: *I promise to love you forever, cherish you for all time (and lose any ability to notice*

that other desirable men still walk the earth), *'til death do us part.*
When David glanced over again, I turned away, always worried
that he could read me like one of his clues.

"The thing is," I said, "other people might ask, *Where's the
gold? How do I get to the treasure?* Not you. You think, *Hmm, if
I were going to make a treasure hunt, here's what I'd do.* You crawl
inside it."

David thumped his fingers on the chicken wire fence. "Maybe,"
he said, dismissing my compliment to focus again on that expanse
of dirt.

At five foot two with fair skin and wavy, light brown hair, I
felt diminutive next to David, who stood a foot taller and probably weighed two of me. More pronounced than our physical
differences, though, was how we operated on opposing energetic
frequencies: mine, antsy, versus his, methodical and unruffled. I
wanted to get started already, find the right spot and start churn-
ing up dirt until the steel edge of the shovel met with the curved
wooden lid of the chest. I could imagine the sound—dense and
slightly metallic, but with a trace of hollowness. *Thunk.* I'd been
waiting for decades to find real treasure and could barely tamp
down my urge to dig, right then, right there. But I had to respect
David's geeky expertise that had led him to winning two major
hunts similar to this one.

So, as he continued to survey the garden, I paced the perim-
eter, curling my fingers into fists and scanning the area for things
left or lost, twinkly or bright, the kind of treasure I'd been finding
all my life. Walking to school as a young girl, I would sweep my
eyes over the pavement, searching for something to deliver me
from my volatile father's unchecked rage, my mother's cool disinterest. If a cheery yellow button or renegade paper clip winked at
me in the sunlight, I would pick it up and slip it into my pocket.
At some point I began to imbue these found things with meaning.
Spotting something green meant go ahead with whatever project

I'd been dreaming up; a heart-shaped stone promised love to come; on the rare occasion when I stumbled upon a lost jewel—a broken gold earring, a runaway bead—I'd feel a surge of connection with my stylish mother who loved high heels and fashion jewelry.

"What are you doing with that piece of junk?" my mother would ask if I dared to show her my discovery. "Cripes. Throw that away before you catch tetanus."

I never did—catch tetanus, or throw it away. I saved everything. Still do.

A ceramic bowl in my office brims with my recent finds: dozens of coins, some shiny round washers, a nugget of fool's gold, and a sharp blue tile, perfectly square. I have an iridescent marble the color of soap bubbles; a pink plastic ring I mined from a patch of ice in the Stop & Shop parking lot one brutal March morning; and, one of my favorites, a brooch crushed by a car tire in a pedestrian crosswalk and flattened into a leaf-shaped mosaic of shattered gemstones.

How did you see that? my son or daughter might ask as I pick up a thumbnail-size piece of sea glass in the tumble of rocks by the ocean's edge or a dirty quarter in the gutter on a dark December night. How? *I'm like a crow,* I tell them, always concealing a bleaker truth: With an instinct born of yearning, I have trained myself to find things. Even as I waited for David, logical in his approach to pretty much everything, I simply hoped some sign would appear amidst the coffee cups trapped by the sieve of a chain link fence and magically point *me* to the treasure chest. It was the same way I once believed a key-shaped soda pull-tab might open the portal to a hidden world, one that would let me walk away from my childhood into a place where no one could hurt me. But no such sign materialized in that moment. Instead, David turned to me with his trademark restraint and said, "I guess we should have a look."

With that, I let out a deep breath and lunged toward the garden gate.

We decided not to haul the two steel shovels from the SUV until we needed them. As for the metal detector purchased from Amazon, David was hoping not to use it at all and return it for a refund. The idea of this hunt was to find money, not blow it on the search. Plus, neither of us had much to blow: he, as the divorced dad of three girls; me, as a writer and part-time college English teacher.

"What *exactly* should I be looking for?" I asked, trailing David through the gate. "Give me specifics."

"Maybe a parrot, or anything having to do with pirates," he reasoned. "There's probably going to be some obvious clue on the site, possibly even a potato plant."

I squinted at him. "What does a potato plant have to do with pirates?"

"I haven't figured that out yet," he said, "but there's a reference to a potato in the first video."

"Okay," I said. "I'll keep my eyes *peeled*."

"Ha!"

As much as I adored David, he terrified me. Practically impervious to flirtation—a rare trait in middle-aged men with a pulse—he guarded his heart with the care of one who had suffered from that organ's fragility. "I don't trust easily," he once confessed, as a way of explaining why he'd been slow to date again after his divorce. Stymied in most attempts to charm my way to closeness with him, I resorted to making asinine jokes that he typically responded to with a fast smile and a chuckle, my best confirmation that he actually liked me. For a guy obsessed with cracking codes, David, admittedly, could be oblivious when it came to deciphering the cryptic nature of women. And despite my concerns that he could read my thoughts, I don't believe he was aware of the feelings he provoked in me or that he sometimes felt like a possible answer to a lengthy stretch of lonely, a problem that was supposed to be fixed by marriage: one person to vanquish years of longing, as if any puzzle could be solved that easily.

For a few minutes I followed behind David as he walked ponderously, neither of us observing anything remarkable. With so much space to explore and limited hours to search before dark, I finally suggested divide and conquer.

"Go for it," David said. "Shout if you see something curious."

"Curious? I'm going to find that treasure chest."

"I wouldn't be surprised," he said, "the way you notice things."

I smiled at him, quietly delighted that he had recognized my talents. I couldn't solve complicated math clues, but I definitely noticed things. I grew up reading the signs of my parents' anger, always tuning in to the timbre of our Catholic household that told me when to hide in my closet or when their moods—heightened by a pitcher of Manhattans—made it safe enough to come out.

I hid things, too. I buried the pieces of myself that my father never saw before he died twenty-six year ago, the same pieces that my eighty-two-year-old mother, who was now hobbling toward death, might also never see. But that was the problem: I didn't know where to look for that lost part of myself. I'd taken to falling asleep at night with one hand on my chest, the other pressed to my gut, trying to touch the unreachable place of desire stirred to life by my mother's advancing illness, and an unexpected awareness of my own mortality. *What is missing that will make me feel whole, and why, when I'm teetering on the brink of fifty, can I still not find it?*

Continuing down the dirt path alone, I scrutinized each garden plot, some of which already had been planted for the season, while almost as many remained barren or choked with weeds. I was supposed to be looking for "on-the-ground clues," as they are called in the armchair treasure-hunting lexicon. More specifically, we needed a crow's nest, pirate ship, and flying birdy, or at least real-world representations of those objects. A few rows over, I noticed that David, his face inscrutable, was staring intently into one of the plots. I stopped and watched him.

David lived in a neighboring Massachusetts town with his daughters, his girlfriend, his mother, and four mostly female pets. A mutual friend, Kathleen, had connected us five years earlier when Sting's wife, Trudie Styler, turned one of my essays into a short film starring Kerry Washington, and I appeared on *The Today Show* to promote it. Around that time David had solved another armchair treasure hunt similar to our Brooklyn one and was getting some interest from Hollywood about turning that story of discovery into an adventure movie. "How do you two celebrities not know each other?" Kathleen asked when she introduced us one morning at school drop-off.

"I love treasure hunting, too," I mentioned to David as the two of us lingered on the playground, exchanging stories of our recent newsworthy experiences. Although I wanted to impress him—a true treasure hunter who had actually found valuable things—I did not elaborate on my belief that things of value appear all around us, if only people would take notice. I certainly didn't reach down to pick up the rhinestone butterfly barrette I'd been eyeing in the damp playground wood chips, at least not until he turned away, and I could bend over and surreptitiously grab it.

I was still staring at David when he signaled me over. "What's that?" He was pointing at some feathery growth in an otherwise empty dirt plot. "Potatoes?"

As the daughter of a father who had lavished his garden with the affection he'd withheld from his daughters, I knew my vegetable plants. "That's asparagus," I said. "It bolts like crazy when the weather warms up. Kind of like kids."

There was that quick smile and chuckle. Not that I noticed or anything.

We continued wandering, this time together, aware of glances from some legitimate gardeners, including a woman battling her sixties with a bottle of peroxide and midnight-blue eyeliner. Holding a cigarette in one hand and a milk jug repurposed as a watering can in the other, she returned our *hello* with a tight nod.

"What's she going to do when we start digging up the pirate's chest?" I whispered.

"I don't know," David said, still peering closely into every plot. "Let's worry about that when the time comes."

But the time wasn't coming, at least not then. When my phone buzzed a few moments later, I forced myself to answer. "Hey," I said.

"How's it going?" Mark asked, his voice cloyingly upbeat. Although we hadn't resolved the tension around this trip, we'd at least sidestepped it for a while. "Did you find anything?"

"Not yet." I wandered out of David's earshot. "It's complicated."

"But you still think you're going to find it, right?"

I looked out at the park, more enormous than anything we could tackle that afternoon without another targeted spot to focus our attention. The word *impossible* leapt to mind, as did *morons*. "We're pretty hopeful," I said.

"Well, that's great. So, I'll see you around seven thirty still? We're meeting Maggie and Pete at eight o'clock."

I squeezed my eyes shut. "You know," I said, with my jaw clenched, "just to be safe, I think we should postpone. Traffic out of the city could be brutal."

When Mark didn't answer, I filled the silence. "I'm sorry," I pleaded. "I thought this would be quick."

"I did, too," he said.

We hung up without our usual "I love you."

"Everything okay?" David asked when he saw me snap my phone shut.

"For some reason," I said, "driving five hours to look for a pirate's treasure chest doesn't make sense to everybody."

David smiled. "Hard to believe, isn't it?"

Though we tried to be strategic after that, David and I ended up darting about in various directions, covering acres of land in search of something that could be our flying birdy clue. At one point, David trekked back to the car to retrieve a shovel and had his way with a patch of weeds. "I came here today to dig and, dammit, I'm going to dig," he insisted, both of us laughing as he jammed the steel edge into the dirt with exaggerated thrusts. When his efforts produced nothing but more dirt, he broke out the metal detector and poked the black sensor head into low clusters of branches.

I used that time to circle a nearby asphalt lot in search of a sign, any sign, stopping when I happened upon a puddle of blue-and-white crockery shards, a broken plate from someone's picnic perhaps. I kneeled to examine the various pieces before choosing a triangular chunk with blue flowers. Though obviously not related to the treasure hunt, it still felt like a clue. "It's here," I told myself. I slipped the triangle into my pocket and rejoined David.

"We probably should quit for today," he said, wiping his forehead with his sleeve and gazing into the shrubs. "I'm getting nothing."

"Seriously?" I couldn't bear the idea of leaving without the chest of gold. "I have a feeling we're close." I touched the piece of pottery, sharp between my thigh and jeans.

"Feelings aren't clues."

I didn't say it, but I thought it: *For me they are. Everything can be a clue. This shard in my pocket. That cloud shaped like a hawk. Us being here on a May afternoon hunting treasure.*

"Let's stay a little longer," I begged. I believed the treasure was in that park somewhere, and I didn't want our day, full of quirky fun and promise, to end that abruptly. I couldn't remember when I had last felt so motivated by anything. "Come on," I pleaded. "We have to find it."

David half smiled. "You are persistent."

We walked in focused silence until we came to the Kings County Fair, one of those honky-tonk operations with bagged cotton candy and sketchy rides yanked off of a few dirty flatbeds. At the makeshift bar in the food tent, David ordered a beer while I guzzled a glass of water and then left the tent and headed across the field, a 1,400-acre conundrum that needed to be solved before dark.

It was coming on twilight, that fleeting time of day that always felt like loss to me. Already I could sense the minutes slipping away to the tinny sounds of a carnival soundtrack.

"Where?" I asked out loud over that monotonous jingle. "Where is the treasure?" Closing my eyes and opening my fists as if catching rain, I lifted my hands over my head, not really caring that I looked like a TV evangelist praising the Lord. "Where?" I asked again, as I had so many times before under wildly different circumstances. As a child, it was, *Where are the parents who are supposed to love me?* Later it warped into, *Where is my life's path? The great adventure? The feeling of wholeness?* I sometimes wondered if *where* was my first word. I just didn't want it to be my last. I'd been looking for that intangible *where* for my entire life, and here I was on a Friday afternoon in a defunct Brooklyn airport, ignoring my children, pissing off my husband, looking again because I didn't know what else to do. *Where? Where? Where?*

I plopped down on the side of a runway in the dry bramble, once wetlands, and waited for an answer. Nothing came. I pinched a bit of dirt between my fingers and brought it to my nose, sniffing deeply for the earthy smell of potatoes or metallic notes of gold dust. Still nothing. I touched the dirt to my tongue until I could taste the dry grit of my father's garden on a long-ago summer day, before spitting it out in disgust for the taste, and myself.

When I returned to the food tent, I found David perched on a barstool inspecting a map of the park. He swished his mouth around as if gargling his thoughts.

"What?" I asked, reading an idea in his eyes.

"Before we go, let's try the North Forty." He pointed to a wooded area a few hundred yards past the fairgrounds.

It was getting dark as we approached the small forest popular with birders and hikers. There was a prominent *Keep Out* sign posted near the entrance, but that didn't stop us from walking right by. "What do you think?" David asked after a few moments, before we reached the thick of the woods.

"Don't know," I said, echoing the doubt in his voice. "Are they really going to bury the treasure in a place we're not supposed to go?"

"The website said no."

We stopped and faced each other. Right behind David, I could sense the rustle of the woods: the indiscernible life and unknowable danger so terrifying to me as a girl. As we stood there, close enough that our breath overlapped in the growing darkness, a police car drove by, drenching us in a shower of headlights. I wanted to seize David's arm and pull him close. But as the squad car began to slow down, my partner in crime spun around and began walking back.

It would be nearly seven o'clock before we drove out of the airfield with the shovel bouncing around in the rear of the truck, no treasure chest to lock it in place. I tried to call Mark, but he didn't pick up. "On my way home," I sang to his voicemail.

When I arrived at my house close to midnight, I went to Phinny's room first and stroked my twelve-year-old's shaggy brown hair, now tossed across his pillow. Phinny always felt far away when he was sleeping, like he'd entered a secret world where no one could find him. In her room across the hall, ten-year-old Addie's closed eyes looked troubled, until I kissed her head and she stirred a bit from the heaviness of a dream. Even in sleep she was easier to reach. Next, I stole into my own bedroom and stripped off my dusty clothes. When I tossed my jeans into the hamper, the pottery shard clunked onto the hardwood floor. I picked it up and set it on my nightstand. After a quick rinse, I slid into bed trying not to wake Mark and reveal the hour of my return. When I felt him shift with my weight on the mattress, I held myself still until his breathing dropped into his chest, and I was once again alone.

Finally, slowly, I drifted into sleep, thinking of that far-off airfield, of clues, of crow's nests, of growing old, of treasure, of that thing I lost long ago—lost, or maybe simply had not yet found.

2 - CLUES

On a Saturday afternoon several months before that day in Floyd Bennett Field, my mother phoned from the hospital.

"What?" I sputtered when she told me she'd spent the night there. "Why didn't you call sooner?"

"I'm fine, Sandy," she assured me, brushing off my worry. "I had a minor stroke and heart attack. The neighbors helped me. Deb is here now." I heard her across-the-street neighbor cheerfully sing out, "Hi, Sandy!" from somewhere in that sterile room where I should have been. Did Deb know how jealous I felt that she was there, likely hanging my mother's white sweatshirts in a narrow hospital closet, or did she think of me as the indifferent daughter who was relieved to have others managing my responsibilities?

"I'll pack a bag and be there in two hours."

"No, Sandy! Don't come!" she insisted. "What are you going to do? Stare at me? Cripes, I'm hooked up to all these tubes." I could picture my easily irritated mother swatting at the IV hose like flies at a picnic.

"But, Ma. I can—"

"Sandy! I said no! I don't *want* you to come. But call Betsy for me, will you?"

I hung up and dialed my sister, who lived in Germany. "Ma's in the hospital," I said, feeling myself tear up, something I could never do in front of my no-nonsense mother, while Betsy, a trained social worker, had an infinite capacity for listening to my heartbreak. Of course, she herself bawled over anything mildly emotional (an old

Barry Manilow ballad on the radio could reduce her to a puddle), unless it had to do with our parents. After sobbing her way through a childhood rife with my mother's emotional neglect, and our long-deceased father's quick-to-catch temper, that well had run dry.

"If she doesn't want you to visit, then don't," Betsy insisted. She had moved to Munich twelve years earlier when she fell in love with Robert, a six-foot-eight-inch German BMW engineer whose job would always keep him on the other side of the Atlantic. Eventually they had two towheaded kids who crawled more deeply into my heart with each summer visit, and a European life that felt achingly far away, because it was. "You know that if you do go down there," Betsy continued, sounding more perfunctory than cruel, "she's just going to make you feel like crap." She paused. I knew what was coming. Burdened with the guilt of being out of the country, she said it nearly every time we spoke. "I feel so terrible that this all falls on you."

"It's fine," I assured her, never fully disclosing my secret truth: that I'd hate to be living overseas right now with no possibility of ever really knowing the woman we both called Ma.

When I hung up the phone, I collapsed against the sofa, wondering how my very own mother was such a stranger to me. She lived two hours away in New Britain, Connecticut, but resisted coming for holidays, preferring to celebrate with her brother and his wife, or close friends, of which she had many. "Not this time, Sandy. I've got other plans." The dozen or so times she visited when the kids were young, her searing judgment of my parenting and blatant disinterest in spending time with her grandchildren caused me weeks of sleeplessness; I'd lie in bed each night reliving every affront, every fight. But all I had with my mother was hope, so when the next holiday rolled around, I'd invite her again, until I had accumulated too many *no's* to bear and, finally, for my own self-preservation, had to stop asking. Beyond the designation of mother and daughter, our most solid connection came through the care packages she sent for birthdays, the most recent containing two pastel T-shirts from T.J. Maxx that I promptly dropped off at the Goodwill, tags still attached. She refused to believe I didn't like pastels. *What do you mean, Sandy? Of course you like pastels! Everyone likes pastels.*

"What do you need?" Mark had asked when I told him that my mother had been hospitalized. He still had both his parents and did his best to support me. But his compassion couldn't fix, or even temper, what was broken between my mother and me. I'd been alone with this struggle for most of my life and didn't know another way of dealing with the wall between us, except to occasionally heave myself against it, wondering if it would ever give way.

"I need for my mother and me to need each other, or something," I wailed. "What if she dies tomorrow? What will I say in her eulogy? That she was an excellent shopper if you're into baby blue T-shirts?"

"And she could work miracles on stains."

"Well, there's that." I hit my fist on the sofa cushion, as if trying to loosen something from the fibers, or maybe the tears that I so seldom shed.

A few weeks after my mother had been released from the hospital back into her life, those tears, almost inexplicably, began to fall. They came out of nowhere one morning as I was heading down the hall to start my writing day. Instead of going to my home office, I crossed the living room and collapsed on the sofa in the stillness. After a while of just sitting there, I began plucking at the worn green upholstery and crying harder. I didn't move, terrified of how the sadness that had been building for years just ambushed me that day, insisting that I acknowledge it.

Finally, with a little self-redirection that always seemed to come in my mother's critical voice—*Honestly, Sandy, what is your problem?*—I staggered to my feet and tried forcing myself to my writing desk. But after a decade of doing exactly that, I collapsed again, this time on the floor. Seconds later my face crumbled, and I began to weep profusely, unstoppably, wet snorting sobs that I could not bring under control. I curled into myself and buried my face in a crimson throw pillow, futilely attempting to contain the wellspring.

When I continued to cry through the morning, I had to question what was happening and if it would ever stop. I heard awakenings sometimes masqueraded as breakdowns and vice versa. Could I be having one? The other? Did I get to choose?

"I don't know what it is," I told Mark on the phone when I caught him between clients. "My heart just started leaking sadness."

Although it didn't take a psychologist to know that things weren't okay, Mark happens to be one. But I never wanted to present as one of his therapy patients, and typically didn't.

By all objective standards my life was good. I had a generous husband who still looked hot in his ten-year-old Lucky Brand jeans, two madcap kids, writing work, a teaching job, and a community of close friends who knew how to rock a potluck. But that's how lives seem sometimes, concealing unspoken wants, making every day, though plentiful with blessings, feel wretchedly lacking. I know much of it had to do with craving my mother's love, but it was knottier than our tangled relationship. Despite all that I had, I still felt like I was made of longing.

Each day I searched for what I believed might lead to my own treasure: clues as varied and scattered as autumn leaves, as tempting as the broken sunglasses that I rescued from the Target parking lot, or the heads-up penny lying on the subway platform. A morning's worth of commuters could ignore that stray bit of copper as easily as I could not. I had to pick it up in case it had something to show me, and it usually did. Each salvaged object held meaning for me, but nothing I found ever felt like enough. Surely that thing I needed existed somewhere on this earth. But where to find it? And how?

Without a string of arrangements, I couldn't leave anymore, not for a weekend, certainly not for a week, never mind the way I once could when the world beckoned, and off I'd trot with a few hundred bucks and my red Samsonite suitcase. By the time I was twenty-five, I'd lived and worked on both coasts and three continents. I'd traveled the world, searching, and I wanted to keep going. Sometimes I couldn't abide how small my world as a wife and mother in the suburbs had begun to feel, and how half of my life—if I had the good fortune of making it to my mid-nineties— had already passed. I could practically touch the hole in my heart, a vessel of want that refused to stay filled.

"I'll be okay," I tearfully assured Mark that day on the phone before hanging up. But it was a lie, the first of many I would tell him. At some point in our brief conversation, I realized I didn't really want his comfort anymore. I wanted to touch whatever oily darkness lurked beneath my tears, the way my childhood friends and I used to poke sticks into the sewer drain and pierce the layers of rotting leaves. I wanted to dredge up that thing that seemed just out of reach, no matter how wretched it smelled.

꩜

"Maybe you're having an existential depression," my spiritual friend Liz said when, still crying, I called her later that afternoon. Liz had been my roommate in college, and then went on to get her master's degree at Yale Divinity School, never relinquishing her New Age streak or sexiness. When my friend Gary met her at my wedding, first in her white clergy robe, then later in a black halter dress at the reception, he leaned in to me and whispered, "She's like heaven and hell rolled into one."

"What do I do?" I asked Liz.

"You let yourself feel it and, at some point, try to connect to the source of your sadness."

I moaned. I couldn't remember when I last connected to anything deeply beyond my kids. Although I journaled every night, documenting the events of my day, even the stream of energy that had once powered my pen had begun to dry up since my mother's health scare weeks earlier. I kept imagining the entry that began: *My mother died today.* And when exactly would I be writing that? Tomorrow? In ten years? And what would I say next? *I didn't even know her. My mother died and now what?*

"I wish I had a mother I could call."

"Try her," Liz said. "Maybe she'll surprise you."

"Oh cripes, Sandy," my mother said that night on the phone when I told her I wasn't feeling well. "You probably have the flu."

"It's not the flu, Ma. It's more like I'm—I don't know—sad."

"Sad?" She actually *harrumphed*. What she lacked in empathy, she made up for in onomatopoeia. "What have you got to be sad about?"

"I don't know."

"Well, you better get over it. You have a family to take care of."

"You know, Ma, sometimes I just want you to say—"

"Say what? What am I supposed to say, Sandy?" she asked. I could hear the flick of the lighter and the first puff, followed by a long, raspy exhale. She had been smoking since age thirteen and wasn't going to quit just because of a little stroke and heart attack. "Now tell me, how are the kids?"

After we hung up, I threw on my son's old winter jacket and started toward the door.

"Where are you going, and when are you coming back?" Mark shouted from the TV room, as if I were dashing out to buy lunch meat rather than reevaluate my life. I answered by slamming the front door behind me, a punctuation trick I'd learned from my mother.

Once outside I headed for the town bike path just a block from our house. I could feel my heart beating out bass notes of fear that I'd be attacked, alone after dark in my Boston suburb. Still I charged along, scanning the asphalt, hoping some clarifying symbol would appear before me. I kept walking, searching, trying to outpace my fear, until the inky black path opened into the muted light of Spy Pond, a popular spot in the area for recreation and reflection. A steady drift of pond visitors plus two million people traveling the bike path annually resulted in plenty of dropped items: beads, game pieces, belt buckles, socks, nip bottles, baby shoes, broken earbuds. I had discovered some of my favorite treasures around that pond, often on solitary evening walks that had begun to stretch into hours.

With my hands in my pockets, I trudged along the dirt toward the water's edge and stepped onto one of the granite boulders. A one hundred-acre kettle hole formed fifteen thousand years ago by the receding Wisconsin glacier, Spy Pond felt as old as time and as dear as that friend who always takes your calls, then patiently listens for the better part of an hour as you babble incomprehensibly. I found a willow branch and skated the flimsy stick over the gunmetal gray surface, disturbing the mirrored illusion of texture and depth.

"What?" I said. "What are you trying to show me?"

The pond listened, as ponds do.

"You don't understand," I whispered. "I want it now."

I squeezed my eyes shut, ashamed of how I had so much, but still felt pressed against the wall of my own longing. What of myself could I still not find, and why did I live in such awareness of the gaps, hoping some great wind might rise up between them and carry me away?

I plunked down cross-legged on a boulder nearly level with the water and stared into the glassy surface like a fortune-teller scrying with her crystal ball. "Tell me," I pleaded. "Tell me where to look." But the water revealed only what was: a glimpse of my hunched-over reflection, my neck and head like a dark keyhole. I wanted to sit and stare for hours until a golden key appeared and opened me up like an answer. But I couldn't stay, of course, not on a weeknight with lunches to prepare, papers to grade, and Mark's worry over where I'd gone. So I gathered myself and stood slowly. As I did, I bent to pick up a glittering speck that, in the spare moonlight, resembled a fallen star. Only I knew from a lifetime of looking that it would be nothing more than a piece of glass, likely from a beer bottle cast off by some high school kid. I typically didn't collect broken glass unless an unusual color or shape struck my fancy, but that small shard became mine, so did the next, and the next and the half-dozen others I found on the ground, as all the way home I searched for pieces of myself.

3 - GUIDE

"Did you find it?" Addie hollered down from her bedroom the morning after I returned from Floyd Bennett Field.

I hesitated before shouting back, "No." As an afterthought, I added, "Sorry." As much as I wanted to find the chest in New York, I knew my children also desperately hoped I would come home like a true pirate, with a pile of gold and a swashbuckling tale.

"Did you find *anything*?" my son called, disappointment deepening his changing voice.

"Nothing," I said, not a fully honest answer. I didn't find a pirate flag, a potato, or a pile of gold, but I did find something. Though it wasn't tangible or shiny, I could feel it, my determination to unearth that treasure. The desire that had swelled inside of me during the trip had less to do with a chest of gold than the experience of discovery, a quest that connected me to great treasure hunters through time: pirates, pioneers, monks, nuns, deep sea divers, writers, artists, and explorers who gave their lives to the search for something bigger than themselves. They were answering a call, and maybe I was, too, the way I once used to pack my bags and leave the country in search of adventure. I could no longer go so far afield, but I had to go somewhere.

I nuked the last of the breakfast sausages and, shouting upstairs, urged the kids into their soccer clothes, tuning in with one ear until I heard them rummaging for shorts and socks in the laundry that hadn't been washed when I was in Brooklyn. While

Mark logged in long hours at a nearby psychiatric hospital, I, with my home office and job flexibility, tended to be the primary keeper of the house—laundress, cook, and cleaner. At one time I had approached these chores halfheartedly, with piles of dirty clothes and general family filth and detritus putting me in the mood to write. Nothing unleashed my creative animal quite like a sink stacked with cereal bowls or a crud-covered kitchen floor. Lately though, a heap of clean laundry had begun to satisfy me in a way that a half-written article no longer could. Four piles of folded shirts sometimes represented the most quantifiable success in the course of a workday.

I was opening the dishwasher when Addie wandered downstairs. Petite, with gray eyes and an uncombed tousle of blonde hair, she was my chance at a longed-for mother-daughter relationship, just in reverse of how I once expected it. Here I was in the grown-up role, loving my heart out, screwing up often, and regularly wanting to plead, *No fair! I don't know how to do this. I need a mother to help me.*

Addie picked up one of her sausages with her fingers and nibbled daintily. A curious mash-up of quirky and shy, she was the kind of kid who regularly wore purple footy pajamas to school then covered her ears and screeched when some well-meaning teacher commented on them. "Isn't that quite the outfit?" they'd say. Cue shrieking.

"Are you going to go to New York again?" Addie asked in her tiny voice.

"Maybe, if we solve some more clues," I said. "I don't really know." But I did know. From the cacophonous center of my suburban life, that treasure felt unreachable, but that sense of loss, or of not having found, only made me more consumed with returning to the ghost airport.

"What did you guys do last night?" I asked, sponging day-old crumbs off the counter.

"Dad ordered pizza," Addie said. "We waited a really long time for you."

Phinny joined his sister at the kitchen island. "Dad was pissed," he said, "real *fucking* pissed." He smiled, devilishly pleased to punish me with his potty mouth, a habit that began when he was seven and we used to take what we called swear walks. I had this novel idea that if Phinny could swear freely in a nonjudgmental environment, he would be disinclined to use those words out in the world. Ah, the best laid plans. This one didn't just backfire, but the proverbial gun blew up in my—pardon my French—fucking face. Phinny didn't just like to swear. He *loved* to swear. He was a one-man swearing band.

"Don't use that word, please," I said.

"Fucking or pissed?"

"Yes."

I studied my son, who was growing out of his boyhood into someone sturdy and angular and, at times, frighteningly beyond my recognition. While marveling at his darkening hair and smart brown eyes, I also searched for the clingy child whose every move I once knew as well as my own. How, right in front of my eyes, was he managing this vanishing act?

"Was anyone else looking?" Phinny asked.

"No one else was there," I told him. "I'm not sure anyone has gotten as far along as we have."

Addie turned to me. "Can I go with you next time?"

"Maybe," I said when I already knew the answer: *absolutely not*. I had always finagled my life and career to fit my mothering, and now I needed that escape to Brooklyn without my children. So that's what I was going to do, if I could just figure out how.

I once read that people who look for treasure might be trying to replace the emotional fulfillment they didn't get when they were young. As I bustled my own children out the door to their soccer games, I had to wonder what, if anything, they weren't getting. I tried to give them everything—my time, my attention, my assurance, my love—because I didn't want them to reach middle age and say, *Where the hell was Mom when we were growing up?* For twelve years I'd been the mother I'd always wanted, prioritizing my children's needs and, in the process, burying my own.

4 - STRUCK

They determined that the murders occurred sometime between 8:15 and 8:45 on the night of October 19, 1974. The worst would have been over as I, a scrawny, bucktoothed nine-year-old, was falling asleep in one of my grandmother's attic bedrooms, with its slanted ceiling and the ghostly scent of mothballs drifting from the closet like memory itself. With my parents at a church social event that night, my sister and I were staying with my grandmother in her rambling, beige house a mile from ours. Had I heard a noise? Gunshots? Police cars? I doubt it. More likely, the scuffed silver radiators that hissed and spit like predators had roused me, prompting me to flee downstairs and crawl into bed with my grandmother. Her skin smelled sweet, scented with cinnamon and cocoa powder like the cookies that always filled the sea-foam green Tupperware container in her pantry. I drew a deep breath and curled into her fleshy warmth.

The next morning the front page of the Sunday *Hartford Courant* featured a photo of police officers gathered in the Donna Lee Bakery, not a half mile away. The headline read: *6 Found Slain in New Britain Bakery*. I had been to the shop once with my father, who sometimes bought us doughnuts after church, and could easily recall the owner's fast smile as he pushed a cardboard box of crullers across the counter. Now he was dead.

The article said the bodies were found grouped in a rear room. One victim's head was almost severed by a gunshot. As I read the article, a voice on my grandmother's yellow radio warned us to lock all doors and windows. *Children should not be out alone. The men are at large, armed and dangerous.*

My grandmother sat down hard in a kitchen chair and took off her glasses. She reached for a paper napkin and patted her forehead. "Oh dear."

"Are we going to be killed?" I asked, reluctant to stand in front of the window in case the murderers were right outside.

"I hope not," she said, then almost as quickly, popped up to gather the ingredients for pancakes. "Flour . . . milk . . . vanilla . . ."

As my grandmother prepared breakfast, I read the article again. I felt myself holding my own head, poking a finger into my temple, shutting my eyes on the unimaginable. Did those people close their eyes while they waited to be shot? Did they watch as it happened? Did they feel themselves die?

When my mother picked us up that morning, she spoke in half-finished phrases. "Who on earth . . . ?" and "Honest to God . . . !" She hustled to the car, a cigarette in one hand, the other pressed over her mouth, while Betsy and I dashed down the walkway, yanked open the car door, and dove onto the bench seat before the murderers, perhaps hiding out in the nearby woods, could shoot us in the head.

That afternoon at home, my mother spoke to her friends in a flurry of phone calls, making connections to the people who had been killed. "Now Sal's friend went to high school with that nice woman who ran in for doughnuts." That was New Britain, a place of intertwined lives, both a college and a factory town, with a colorful weave of mostly Polish, Italian, and Puerto Rican immigrants clustered into neighborhoods that contained a package store, a Catholic church, a "druggie house," and a bakery.

With everyone in a state of high alert, the day dragged on, endless and eerie with no news of an arrest. Hours later, when the night had settled over us like a pall, my father rechecked the doors and windows before bed, yet nothing about those locks felt safe enough to keep out a couple of determined killers. Sometime near midnight when I still hadn't fallen asleep, I crept down the hallway barely illuminated by the thin yellow beam of a night-light and perched on the step stool that had been left beside the closed door to my parents' bedroom. Though I yearned to go in, I knew better. I also knew that when (not if, but when) the killers broke in, I'd be ready. I would wake my parents and sister and lead them through my bedroom window onto the roof. We would hurl ourselves into the branches of my father's blue spruce just a leap from the house, then run to the neighbor's door. We would *not* be shot in the head.

At some point in the night I must have dozed off, because I woke up on the carpet, the metal step stool tipped on its side. My father, most likely awakened by the clatter of my fall, stood over me. "What kind of malarkey is this?"

"Good Lord, Sandy!" my mother said, bursting from the bedroom door behind my father. "I thought it was those bakery guys coming to shoot us." She yanked me up from the floor and shoved me back into my room. "Now stay in there before I give you a crack!" She pulled the door shut hard.

Squeezing my knees together to keep from trembling, I sat on the edge of my twin bed, panicked that just the sound of my breathing might bring my mother in to fulfill her threat. After a while when I was still alone, I opened my gold jewelry box brimming with cheap pins and rings and necklaces and dozens of found things. There was the fuzzy heart key chain I'd swiped from the floor of the bank and, under that, a granite arrowhead discovered in a nearby field. With a bit of quiet stirring, I excavated the four gold cross necklaces I had received five years earlier as First Communion gifts and, slipping each from its slinky chain, arranged them in a row on my nightstand. Then I prayed: *Dear God, don't let them kill us.*

In a way, my childhood scavenges had been inspired by the

Catholic Church, which gave sanctified meaning to so many things—objects, colors, even gestures. White stood for Christ; green for rebirth. Incense rode our prayers to heaven, while a crucifix signified Jesus dying for our sins. And the flat, round wafer that we so reverently chewed at the end of each Mass did not just symbolize Jesus Christ, but actually *became* Jesus Christ.

I was in first grade the day I learned about transubstantiation in a dank basement of St. Francis of Assisi Church. *How is that possible?* we kept asking Father Clancy, our after-school religion teacher who was preparing us to make our First Holy Communion. *Really, the bread actually turns into Jesus?*

But like a magician who would never reveal his tricks, Father Clancy just kept insisting, "Yes indeed! That's God up there on the altar."

From that point on, I waited for that critical moment in church each week when the priest would raise the plate of bread and the gold chalice of wine and declare them to be the body and blood of Jesus Christ. I wanted a sign that it was true, perhaps a trickle of blood down the mirrored golden cup in confirmation of my wobbly faith. But no. As I kneeled there, hands clasped, eyes popping with focus, trying not to miss the moment, I never once witnessed any physical manifestation of Jesus Christ on that altar. Still, I learned to believe in the transformative magic of everyday objects. If that tasteless piece of bread could turn into God right before my eyes, then my found things could be transcendent, too.

In the days after the murder, Betsy and I walked the quarter mile to Stanley School and back, trying to achieve that edge of fast walking and almost running, aiming to be neither shot in the head nor labeled weird for the way we moved—two equally horrible fates for any kid to suffer. In an effort to keep our route streamlined, we calculated each step, cutting across the church parking lot to minimize exposure to the murderers.

More interested in getting to school and back alive, I didn't look for treasure in my typical way. But that didn't stop me from seeing it in front of the Getty Station: a red lighter, as bright as blood against the sidewalk. Fearing a trap, I didn't pick it up. Maybe the murderers had put it there, and whoever touched it first would be shot in the head. Still, even as Betsy and I strode past it, my fingers ached to grab that lighter, a strongly felt clue, but for whom? I thought about it all morning, through reading group that I excelled in and math class that made me have to go to the bathroom. I could almost feel the smooth camber of the plastic against my palm and smell the warm flame, slightly redolent of butane. Why hadn't I taken that lighter, and what if someone else had picked it up already?

By 11:30 I was sweating as I watched the minute hand of the clock, so slow it seemed to be broken. At noon when the lunch dismissal bell clanged, instead of waiting for Betsy, I dashed out of the schoolyard, pushing through the crowd of kids clustered in front of the chain-link gate. As I ran toward the Getty Station, I felt a heave of relief in my chest when I spotted my red lighter from almost a block away. I swooped like a hawk with talons extended, snatched it up, and kept running, still not convinced that I wouldn't be killed. I ran my fastest, across the church lot, up Pendleton Road, my fingers sore and damp from gripping so hard. When I burst through the door, my mother turned quickly. "What's the matter? Someone chasing you?" I darted upstairs and stashed the lighter in an empty Buster Brown shoebox in the back of my closet. Then I went down to the kitchen and quietly ate my egg salad sandwich and fruit cocktail, hoping Betsy would make it home alive, too.

Later that afternoon, I sat in my bedroom, thumbing the lighter's tight metal wheel, working up the courage to strike hard enough to force a flame. Slowly it filled me with a small, reassuring heat. When I began to worry that my mother would discover it in my closet and accuse me of smoking—as plenty of grade school kids did in the seventies—I scurried around my room gathering the dozens of other things that I had collected in my wanderings: beach stones and sun-bleached shells arranged in tidy piles on my bookshelves, baubles in my jewelry box, a bowl filled with coins, and a small wooden treasure chest of plastic charms from the penny gumball machine outside the A&P. One by one, I added them to the shoebox in my closet: my first trove.

The nights that followed those long days after the murders had an amorphous quality as I floated in and out of sleep, often jerked awake by a screeching car or drunk teenagers kicking around our neighborhood of respectable two-story homes and yards full of old-growth trees that could easily conceal two criminals. When the house was silent, and I thought terror alone might kill me, I would take out my red lighter and let that small fire burn away my fear.

On October 29, ten days after the murders, I turned ten. In the one photo I am an awkward girl blowing out pink candles on a frosted cake that my grandmother had made from scratch. I don't remember much else about that birthday, except a single wish fulfilled three weeks later when two men were officially charged with the crime. The stories and evidence that emerged over the following months, then at the trials, captivated me, indeed the entire state, but only after the men were sent to jail did I feel safe enough to wander beyond the confines of my yard. My preferred place of escape was The Brook, a waterway that cut a narrow swath through our neighborhood until it channeled into a cement tunnel with a dank, forbidding smell. Where it led beyond the tunnel, I didn't know, but The Brook always gave me a feeling of belonging to something bigger in the world, and I would spend whole afternoons looking for treasure in the form of pebbles, bottle caps, and fallen scrolls of birch bark along the wooded banks.

That summer when I was ten, Betsy and I wrote a message with our address on a piece of pale-blue stationery then rolled it into a clear-glass soda bottle. Using my red lighter to melt a handful of broken crayons, we sealed the entire bottle with a protective layer of rainbow-colored wax, and then we brought it down to The Brook. Standing on a large granite boulder that we had christened Treasure Island, we ceremoniously launched the bottle into the churn of the current, hoping that in a month or two someone from faraway would find it and write back. No one did, but for years afterwards I would think about that bottle. Was it still in the cement tunnel unable to escape New Britain? Had it survived the journey into the world? Or had it shattered into pieces, leaving behind a trail of broken shards?

5 - BEACON

The Saturday after my Floyd Bennett failure with David, I sat in front of my computer googling armchair treasure hunts.

I learned how, in 1979, a guy named Kit Williams had self-published a clue book called *Masquerade* that sent people darting around the English countryside in search of a small, golden hare that the author had crafted himself. Thus, the concept of armchair treasure hunting was born. Although someone eventually found the 18-karat gold statue, other hunts have remained unsolved for decades. For example, in 1982, a Brooklyn man named Byron Preiss buried twelve keys in public parks across the United States and then released a related book of clues called *The Secret*. Anyone who uncovered a key could exchange it for one of the twelve jewels that Preiss had selected as prizes. When Preiss died unexpectedly in a car crash in 2005, only two keys had been dug up, but, according to the online article, people still obsess over finding the remaining ten.

I clicked back on the website for our treasure hunt, wondering again what leads David had missed and how I could help to solve them.

That's when I looked up to see Mark in the doorway of my office. His hands were stuffed in his pockets, forcing his shoulders into a shrug of indifference. Although he had accepted my apology for "misjudging the timing" on the Brooklyn trip, discussions about it still held a charge.

"Come over here," I whispered.

He walked behind me and cautiously dabbled his fingers on my shoulders. I reached up and touched the back of his neck, feeling where the fuzz of his salt-and-pepper hair met the frayed collar of a T-shirt, always a surprise and always familiar after eighteen years together.

"The kids are away for a while," he murmured, testing carefully, as one might with a toothpick in a warm cake, hoping I was ready to be taken out and tasted.

"Are they now?" I said.

"Yes, they are," he replied flirtatiously, "but, as you can see, I'm here."

There was a time not long ago when these rare windows with both kids out found us bolting like lovesick teenagers up the stairs and down the hallway to our purple bedroom. Mark would plunge us onto the bed, where we rolled around with longing, both easy and astounding, a steady beat of mutual desire as simple as hunger; the song of our bodies felt like a secret code, the fingerprint of our marriage that no one else could replicate. And while my desire for Mark still surfaced, in recent months fear had accumulated in that hole in my heart, affecting me, affecting us. The comfort I found in his arms had begun to feel like the default path of wife and mother, the route I thought I was supposed to follow, but the very same one that seemed to be derailing me.

My day in Floyd Bennett Field taught me something: I could not stay here in my life exactly like this and still get what my soul was longing for. I needed to go back to Brooklyn and search.

Mark looked over the top of my head at the computer screen. "What's this?"

"A pirate video," I said casually. "I'm trying to figure out what we might have missed."

My husband drew his hands away, leaving my shoulders feeling chilled. "Are you and David planning another trip?"

"No. No." I waved him off. "I mean, if we unlock some more clues and are completely sure about the location, then maybe."

"But you were so sure last week."

"Yeah, but that turned into more of a reconnaissance mission," I said, piling on the nonchalance. "Now that we know the layout of the park and stuff, it should be easier to narrow down the exact spot."

"I see." Mark turned to leave. "I think I'm going to take a nap. I didn't sleep well last night . . ."

He didn't have to finish the sentence for me to know what it was. ". . . waiting up for you."

After a few moments, I turned off the screen and marched upstairs to where Mark, fully dressed in jeans and one of his ubiquitous black fleece vests (he had more black fleece vests than I had bras), was lying on top of our paisley comforter staring up at the angled ceiling. This architectural feature of our bedroom, I recently learned from a *feng shui* video, was the energy equivalent of sleeping under swinging daggers, and with Mark's hands folded behind his head in a stubborn unwillingness to turn and look at me, those corners did seem to be putting sharp edges and bad juju between us.

"Hey," I said and lay down on my back next to him.

"You going to tell me what's going on?" Mark asked. He typically vacillated between an endearing combo of bombast and therapeutic gentleness. Sometimes he cared for me with quiet regard, other times in a loud, Italian, I-know-best way. In the latter case, he would acquire an accent, as if auditioning for Brando's role in a remake of *The Godfather*. This was one of those times: *You gonna tell me what's goin' on?*

"Nothing's going on," I lied. But how was I supposed to explain the messages encoded in my heart: *Keep looking. Don't let anything stop you this time.*

"That's not how it feels."

When I rolled over and faced the window, my gaze floated to the dappled light and shadows dancing through the twisted limbs of the mulberry trees that divided our yard from the town's community garden, a mere fraction in scope of the one David and I had unsuccessfully explored the day before. I scanned the branches for crows, as I had since I was a child, always looking for the one that took those pieces of my heart, imagining that in some mystical way, she was still circling my world with that stone in her beak, waiting for me to recognize her. "I guess I am a little distracted," I admitted. "It's the treasure hunt."

"That was last week. You've been distracted for months."

"It's worse now. I thought we were going to find it. I was so sure."

"You really think you were close?"

"Well, that's the thing," I said, rolling back to face my husband, relieved to be discussing the hunt, as if it—and not my mother, frustration, middle age, and ceaseless longing—were the real problems. "It felt so crazy close, like how could it not be here? But then it wasn't, or we overlooked some major sign."

Unable to resist, Mark began to sing one of his favorite oldies in my ear. "*Sign. Sign. Everywhere a sign. Blockin' out the scenery, breakin' my mind—*"

"As I was saying," I cut him off, "we were missing a sign pointing us to the treasure."

Mark sighed. In his clinical work he probed for answers to alcoholism, abandonment, self-hatred. With my musings, he wasn't terribly inclined to question, perhaps knowing that I did enough self-inquiry without him.

"Do you ever feel called by something?" I asked after a long silence.

"What are we talking about now?" Mark asked. "Signs? Gold? Treasure?"

"Yes," I said. "All of the above, and something bigger, too."

"I'm happy," he said. "I'm not looking for something else."
After a moment he asked, "Are *you* looking for something else?"

"Not really." I turned around to face the fading sunlight, to try
and catch a glimpse of what was out there, waiting for me to finally
uncover it.

6 - AFLOAT

Clutching the metal detector in one hand and a Frisbee in the other, David had anticipated that the security dude playing NASCAR on the nearly empty roads running through Floyd Bennett Field might stop to question what exactly we were doing. In which case, we had a plan.

"As soon as anyone official looks our way," David said, "I'll toss you the disc."

"Okay," I said. "I mean the fact that we're digging for buried treasure on National Park Service property might raise suspicions, but as soon as the cops know we're Frisbee players, well, they'll have to back off."

David laughed. "Point taken," he said, "but it's all we have for cover right now."

While David pressed on through the tall weeds, I stopped to watch a security car cruise past about twenty yards away, then just as quickly circle back in our direction. As the daughter of two punishing Catholic zealots, I grew up believing that I was born into sin and, subsequently, was always doing something forbidden. In this case, I wasn't but still felt guilty. I let the shovel and trowel fall to the ground.

"Hey, David," I called. "Toss it!"

David put down the metal detector and turned to deliver a forehand pass that I caught with the rubbery pink gardening gloves I had grabbed from my shed that morning. I continued to clutch the Frisbee as the guard turned and whizzed by again. When the car had nearly vanished from sight, David and I shrugged at each other. We were either above suspicion or appeared too ridiculous for anyone to ask why a middle-aged couple was playing Frisbee knee-deep in weeds on a Saturday morning, one of us wearing pink gloves.

Even on a weekend when Brooklyn dog walkers should have been out in multitudes, the massive park lacked bustle and life, and that same tang of emptiness sharpened the air, perhaps even more so with the Kings County Fair packed up and gone. David drove us to the nearby baseball fields where we were investing our—well his—most recent code-cracking efforts.

A clue in the final video revealed a picture of the pirate ship with a sign marked "Home Sweet Home." So, David figured "home" could be home plate as in a baseball diamond, of which there were two in Floyd Bennett Field. It aligned with all of the other evidence we'd collected, giving David hope, which in turn gave me hope.

In heading to the baseball fields, we came upon another area with what looked to be a fifty-foot wooden climbing tower strung with a mishmash of ropes. Because of the park's sprawl, we hadn't seen the area on our inaugural trip.

"What is it?" I studied the odd structure that had no easily discernible use.

"Probably some kind of training thing for the Armed Forces Reserve Center around here. Or," David paused and smiled broadly, realization dawning, "maybe it's our crow's nest."

As I continued to examine the tower with sides like ladder rungs on a ship, I saw exactly what he meant. "Of course it's our crow's nest clue," I said, scanning for an actual crow that I would take as confirmation. None appeared, but other clues did.

Within view of the maybe-crow's nest, we found our two base-ball diamonds. Starting at "Home Sweet Home" plate of the larger one, we unwound our 250-feet of twine (a number that came up in the video), until we had measured ourselves into that high patch of weeds.

David nodded. "This feels pretty right."

"Yeah?"

"Yeah."

David took out the metal detector, settled the headphones over his ears, and began sweeping the area as systematically as one can in such thick growth. I scouted around, clutching the Frisbee and keeping an eye out for security guards, but also watching David as he continuously got random clinks from cans, rusted pieces of old pipe, soda tabs, and bottle caps that he then picked up and tossed away.

That went on for several minutes before I heard him shouting for me. "Sandra!"

I whipped around to see my unflappable friend yanking his earphones from the metal detector's jack, causing a furious, loud, insistent firing of beeps, as if the noise couldn't get out fast enough. From across the field we exchanged the briefest glance, an understanding passing between us.

This is it.

I waded through the grass to where David was struggling to shut off the unwieldy gadget. When he finally managed to kill the power, silence struck like a blow. In that silence, every untold possibility for my life began to bloom: I saw a blockbuster film starring Tina Fey, a pirate duet with Jimmy Fallon, and a story my son would die to tell his middle school buddies:

Then my mom, like, dug up this fucking unbelievable pirate chest!

Seriously? That's so cool, dude.

Even *my* mother would have to be impressed. Gold. I had finally struck gold. In less than an hour she'd be phoning her friends. *"Turn on Channel 3, Barb. Sandy found some gold thing!"*

I pulled the trowel from the back pocket of my jeans and shoved it into David's hand. "Dig," I said. "C'mon!"

David looked at me, a little skeptical, not unlike how Mark had looked at me the night before, propped against a pillow on the opposite side of our king-size bed, the space in between like the Gulf Stream, creating a hostile cooling pattern throughout the large room.

"David solved some more clues," I'd said, glancing up from my laptop. "He wants to go back to Brooklyn on Saturday. And . . ."

"And?"

"And," I'd told him with a steely calm, "I want to go with him."

Mark narrowed his eyes. "This Saturday? You're kidding?"

"I'm not."

"Both kids have their final games that day, and we're hosting Addie's soccer party."

"Maybe somebody else can host this time?" I cautiously proposed.

"We volunteered, remember? And since I'm one of the coaches, us hosting makes sense."

I turned back to my laptop and stared at David's e-mail: *Unlocked some more clues. Brooklyn on Saturday. Leaving early. You in?*

"You don't care, do you?" Mark said, shaking his head.

"Of course I care!" I turned to face my husband, so he could read the sincerity in my eyes. "It's just that there will be dozens of soccer parties, and this is a one-time thing."

"Two times in two weeks, if you go."

"But we'll find the treasure, and that will be it."

"You were going to find it last time."

I hesitated, because what I wanted to say sounded idiotic: *This isn't just a treasure hunt. I don't know exactly what it is, but I need this more than I can explain.* Instead I pursued the statistical route. "We don't know how many other people are seriously involved in this thing, but from the online forum, it looks like hundreds," I said. "According to different posts we've seen, some are even lurking around our same path."

"And David is absolutely sure he's right this time?"

"He must be, but we won't know until we look. And if we don't go, someone else will get there first."

Mark peered at me over his glasses, his eyes blazing. Suddenly he was my father ordering me to stop being selfish, my mother telling me, *You're a brat, Sandy, but you can sure be nice when you want something.* After a moment he picked up his magazine again. "Fine. Go! You always do what you want anyway."

"That's not true! I've done what this family has needed for twelve years, and to be fair, so have you. Honestly, how many soccer games have I missed? Two? Three? I love watching the kids play. You must know that."

Mark didn't bother to lift his head. "That's not the point."

"Then what is the point? That we can't do something for ourselves now and then, if it conflicts with a family activity or inconveniences the kids?"

"It's fine," he said in a cleanly measured tone that sliced through a few arteries and ventricles, disconnecting my heart from the rest of my body so I felt nothing but a jarring separation. "Just go!"

I stared for another few seconds at David's e-mail. Then I hit *reply*.

⌒

So here we were, David kneeling in the grass, with me squatting next to him. Finally, he drew a deep breath and jammed the metal tip of the trowel into the earth.

Clink.

I gasped. Fearful of breaking the shared spell of hope we had cast, I kept my gaze trained on the dirt, while David tipped in the trowel a second time and chipped up a small tuft of hard sod tangled with weeds. He did that again, then again, neither of us speaking. Finally, he overturned a big enough clump to reveal a bumpy gray slab. He tapped the ground several feet in every direction, each time getting a dead-sounding clink.

I swallowed hard. "Concrete?"

"Yeah." The trowel drooped as he squinted up at the darkening sky. "It must be an old enclosure for something—"

"But the beeps—"

"Probably a metal lining. Or maybe pipes."

I didn't say much more, trying to keep belief afloat in that deserted airfield, pretending away my devastation.

And, honestly, how often is hope like that? How often do we believe we have found the exact right situation, person, career? How often do we think this must be it, because we have so carefully calculated and planned? We stick a trowel in and get a clink. *This is definitely it,* we tell ourselves. Until, all at once, it isn't.

David and I sat quietly, deflated. Dark rain clouds hung low, diminishing our world even further. More than I hated the gradual acceptance of disappointment, I hated that moment in which belief fizzled before your eyes, and you had to adjust from a place of high expectation to plain old dirt.

"I heard the beeping . . ." David said. "And I thought . . ."

"I know," I said, shushing him. "I know."

I imagined myself telling Mark and the kids how close we'd come, or thought we'd come. Again. But for me there was no joy in *almost,* not when I'd blown another day in Brooklyn instead of helping to host my daughter's soccer party. How was I supposed to justify this or make the case for coming back? More importantly, I owed my mother a visit since I hadn't gone down in over a month, but I wanted to find the treasure first, as if a pile of gold would remedy everything. Didn't she like me better when there was something tangible to brag about? Although none of my successes seemed to impress her that much, I knew she couldn't stay aloof if I showed up on the evening news having found gold in New York City.

I stood and started walking toward an old hangar building and then rounded the corner to where David couldn't see me. I sat down in the weeds with my back against the brick.

"Shit," I said. "Shit. Shit. Shit."

"What are you going to do with the money when you find it?" Phinny, always an early riser, had asked that morning as I brewed my French Roast for the road.

"I only want to keep a few coins," I had told him. "David's done the bulk of the code work, so he deserves the prize. I'm just the apprentice here."

"So why are you doing it?" Phinny settled onto a stool with a bowl of leftover spaghetti. "I mean, if you're not going to get the money?"

I looked at my boy, who, more than anyone I knew, put his arms around life and hugged hard. He didn't make up problems that didn't exist or stress the way kids have learned to do in order to compete and acquire. He was a content, generous soul with a bit of a swearing problem.

"My whole life I've wanted to dig for treasure." I filled my travel mug to the brim with coffee and rifled through the pantry for some granola bars. "Just the experience of looking for that chest is like gold to me."

"Oh," he said, his mouth crammed with pasta. "The only thing that I think is gold, is gold."

I trailed my hand through the patch of weeds that I was sitting in, trying not to think how I'd explain this next failure to Mark, or where my longing had begun to lead, like twine that was tugging me away from him, into this strange place with David. I squeezed my eyes shut in order not to see what I was doing.

After a while David wandered around the corner and sat down next to me. I could feel the heat of his closeness.

"You okay?"

"Yep." Determined to find it that day, I forced myself to my feet. "Let's keep looking."

We explored two more viable spots near home plate, but neither gave us a thing, not even a clink. That low bank of dark clouds was starting to spit rain, and, though it was still early in the day, we had already run through our best possibilities for where the treasure might be buried.

Finally, we ducked into David's truck just as the rain started down in torrents, and thunder shook the air. "You know what?" David said, listening through the rain. "Maybe there's a Morse code thing in the thunder and lightning."

I looked at him quizzically, and then out the window at the sparking sky. "How *exactly*," I asked, "would a bunch of pirate puppets make that happen?"

"In the video!" he said. "There's lightning and thunder in the final video. It could have a code written into it." He reached for his phone and held it between us.

With our heads almost touching, we sat in David's Honda in a nearly empty parking lot in the drenching rain in Brooklyn watching a pirate video on David's four-inch iPhone screen. Straining to hear through the white noise of the real storm, we tried counting short booms as dots and the long ones as dashes, and then attempted to translate those symbols into letters and words. After forty-five minutes, we had produced a handwritten page of dots and dashes that spelled absolutely nothing.

David handed me the paper covered in Morse code. "I give up," he said. "And I'm exhausted." With that, he reclined in his seat and dozed off so comically fast that I laughed out loud. Then I called Mark.

"How was the party?" I asked.

"Fine. Why are you whispering?"

I looked over at David, his hands folded over his chest that rose and fell with the heave of his snoring.

"No reason."

"How's the treasure hunt going?"

"The rain isn't helping."

"But you're going to find it?"

"We're trying."

When I hung up, I let my head fall against the cold, damp glass of the window. I thought of myself, so small inside that car, while out there was a huge empty field. Somewhere in the immensity of that field, under the ground, buried in the dirt, I knew there was a chest filled with gold coins.

Find it, Sandy, I told myself. *Find the treasure.*

7 - HEARD

The following Saturday, I visited my mother in Connecticut. She still lived alone in my childhood house with four bedrooms, the closet in each stuffed to bursting with, among a few pastel-colored clothes, about fifty white button-down shirts and dozens of pairs of crisp white pants neatly doubled over wooden hangers.

"Is your mother a chef or something?" my friend Lisa had asked when she once spent a night with me there.

I laughed. My sister and I had always accepted her mostly monochromatic wardrobe as just another sign that she was nuts, but maybe she was actually working as a short-order cook at the Pancake House. When I once asked my mother why she bought so many of the same white clothes, she brushed me off. "What do you mean by white clothes? Where do you come up with these ridiculous questions, Sandy?"

That Saturday my mother, dressed in light-blue, old-lady jeans and a white sweatshirt, greeted me at the kitchen window with a wave. I pushed the door open.

"Hey, Ma."

"Hey, yourself."

I dropped my bag on the table and reached to hug her. She always had been thin (except for the year she tried to quit smoking and substituted Mr. Goodbars for her Tareytons), but now she had the boniness of a picked-over roast chicken, with hardly a shred of white meat left on her five-foot-four frame. What she did still have was an ageless platinum poof that, for her entire adult life, had never looked uncolored or un-coiffed.

"What's up?" I said.

"Nothing, Sandy. Nothing's up."

"Then let's go to lunch," I suggested. "I just need to pee first."

"Sandy!" she shouted as I started toward the stairs. "Where do you think you're going? Use the bathroom down here!"

"I like the upstairs one better."

"Well, too bad. I want you to use this one! There's nothing wrong with the downstairs bathroom."

My mother was right, but that didn't keep me from scooting up the beige carpeted stairs two at a time. Since she could no longer climb those stairs in under three minutes—cautiously hauling herself up the railing, stopping halfway up to catch her breath—I was assured a few moments of privacy and went straight to her bedroom where I yanked open the drawer to her nightstand.

As a girl, this is where I used to look for clues to my mother. Given an afternoon alone in our two-story colonial, I would slide open the pale wood drawer of her Danish modern nightstand and plunge my hand into piles of socks, maybe excavating a nail file or those stretchy white gloves she wore at night to keep her Vaseline-coated hands from greasing up the pillow. I also found hairnets, bobby pins, and cheap paperbacks that provided me with—when I skimmed through in search of key scenes—a titillating supplement to our bare-bones, elementary school sex education class taught by a sensible, middle-aged teacher named Mrs. Hott.

But really, as much as I appreciated the eye-opening insights culled from those pages, I dug into my mother's stuff for the hope of finding one thing: my mother. I wanted some obvious sign that she was concealing something vitally important, maybe a secret identity that would help to explain her emotional remove. Could she be an FBI informant in a witness protection program or an undercover journalist forbidden from revealing her true self, even to her very own family? It physically pained me that I could never reconcile happy, funny, public Betty, whom her friends adored, with mean, private, flip-your-shit Betty and her zero tolerance for emotion, closeness, and dirt, often coming as a triple threat. *What the hell are you crying about, Sandy? Cripes. You're acting like a baby. And take off those shoes before you track mud all over the floor.*

Around her friends, my mother's ability to laugh at anything read as fun and gregarious. *Isn't Betty a blast?* people enthused. When it was just our family, my mother's mood typically switched to mean, judgmental, and even destructive. *What is her problem?* Betsy and I used to say as she plowed through each room, throwing, tossing, stomping, banging, slamming, and complaining that we were ungrateful slobs. We didn't go to her with any personal needs because we'd only be laughed at or humiliated. I had my period for three months before she discovered I'd been taking pads from the linen closet. "How long has this been going on?" she asked accusingly. "Why do you always hide things from me?"

~

As I rummaged through my mother's nightstand that Saturday afternoon, I realized that nothing had changed since my last visit. I found the usual fuzzy white socks, a squished tube of Nivea, and three pink curlers partly responsible for her miracle hair (the other part was good genes and her hairdresser, Frankie at the Golden Touch Salon). I closed that eternally disappointing drawer and opened the top drawer of her bureau, checking on the one reliable treasure I'd been aware of for twenty-five years, since her mother died.

I sprang open the hinged burgundy box and slipped on my grandmother's engagement ring—a gold band thinned from sixty-two years of wear, topped with a tiny round diamond set in a sparkly square of silver. A folded scrap of paper tucked inside the lid read "For Sandy." Thirteen years ago, my mother had given her own more substantial engagement ring to Betsy on her wedding day, and I often wondered why she held this one back from me when I married Mark in 1997. Perhaps she thought I was too careless with precious things or, based on my penchant for picking up trash, didn't properly value them. Or maybe she felt that I, as the "bratty" daughter, wasn't deserving of something so meaningful. There was nothing in that house I coveted more than my grandmother's ring, and obviously it was intended for me, but I had come to assume that I'd only actually get it over my mother's dead body. I imagined that, after her death, Betsy and I would have the job of sorting through these drawers, and I would finally claim my birthright. But what would such a haphazard hand-off imply? That someday I'd have the treasure, but I'd never have my mother?

Trying to shake off that thought, I briskly removed the ring and returning the box to its place. Then I went downstairs and used the bathroom.

"Now, Sandy," my mother said as I came out buttoning my jeans, "I thought you used the upstairs bathroom."

"I forgot."

"You mean to tell me you went upstairs to use the bathroom, and then you forgot to use it?"

"Yup," I said. I no longer agonized over those polarized inclinations I felt as a child to either behave scrupulously around her or simply say *screw it* and rebel. In fact, most days I felt very little for my mother, who could be hysterically funny with Betsy and me, cracking jokes and making hilarious observations, but always at the cost of real closeness. Even when we were young, she often presented as a fun mom, quick with a saying that would crack me up. "She could eat peanuts off his head," she'd quip to describe a short guy with a taller woman. Or, if someone was wearing an oversized shirt: "They must have bought that at Eddy's Awning Shop." Betty, as I called her when *Ma* felt too intimate, played one of two channels around us: funny or furious. She had no patience for the in-between: the sympathetic listening, the emotional connection, the actual act of mothering two daughters who needed someone to care about them. As a girl I mostly hated to be around my mother, always anticipating the channel switch. And because it still happened when something stirred her up, I typically aimed for neutrality on our afternoons together. Often I'd be sitting across from my mother, the two of us sharing a pizza, and she would seem like some pleasant old lady that I took to lunch now and then as part of a volunteer job at the Senior Center.

"So where to?" I asked. "What do you feel like eating?"

"Oh, I don't care. I'm not even that hungry."

Sometimes we went to the Burger King takeout window for Whopper Jrs., though my mother tended to press for the Captain's Table, once the Donna Lee Bakery where the six people were murdered on that October night in 1974. "They do very nice eggs, Sandy."

"Ma," I'd have to tell her every time, "I can't eat in a place where people had their heads blown off."

"Cripes. You'd think it happened to you."

That day, without her approval, I just drove to an Indian buffet in West Hartford.

"I don't know what I'm eating," she said as I set down the plate that I had fixed for her. She squinted at the selection of curries, naan, tandoori chicken, and bright yellow rice seasoned with turmeric. "Sandy, what is this stuff? Why is this chicken pink?" She chased a piece of food with her fork until she eventually managed to stab it and take a bite.

"How is it?" I asked.

"Pink," she said, laughing.

"You like pink, though."

"For clothes, not chicken." She chewed with her mouth open, dentures clicking. "Tell me what you've been up to?" she said. "I haven't seen you in ages."

"Well, I've been doing some treasure hunting."

"Hunting?" she said too loudly. Nearly deaf, even with Bionic Woman–strength hearing aids, it was impossible to be out with my mother and not attract attention for the vociferous exchanges in which multiple words had to be clarified and repeated. Certain words, with their soft sounds, disappeared completely. Apparently "treasure" was one of them.

"I've been treasure hunting," I repeated, mouthing the words in an exaggerated way. "Treasure. Like pirate treasure. Treasure. TREASURE!"

"Sandy, I don't know what you're saying. This background noise drives me out of my mind." She squinted accusingly around the quiet, nearly empty restaurant before leaning further over her plate and cupping an ear with her hand. "Did you say you're hunting something?" She tapped one of her hearing aids and scrunched up her face, listening hard. I suddenly realized how many ways she had already slipped out of life, beyond the ways she had always been gone. We had never really heard each other.

"Treasure hunting!" I was nearly screaming now. I set my fork on the side of my plate and made a *T* sign with my hands. "*T* as in treasure." The young Indian couple smiled from five tables away. I rolled my eyes as if to say, *Deaf mom. Whatever.*

Our waiter came over to check on us, most likely alarmed by the sheer volume of the conversation that accompanied our boisterous game of charades. "How is your meal so far?"

"Great," I told him.

"It's very good!" my mother shouted. "But I don't know what I'm eating." She laughed. People loved my mother for her big, unedited laugh, but they never had to face the angry backside.

"Well, ma'am," the waiter said solicitously, "please allow me to help." He proceeded to systematically explain each item on the plate while my mother giggled into her napkin.

When he turned away, my mother looked at me, still laughing. "He thinks I don't know what rice is!"

"Ma! Shh! You're screaming."

She waved me off and speared another piece of chicken. "You're so worried about everything."

"I'm not worried," I said, looking around. "I'm embarrassed."

"Well get over it. Now tell me again, Sandy," she said, leaning closer. "What was that *T* word?"

I dug around in my bag for a small notebook that I seldom wrote in anymore, except to make grocery lists or jot down reminders: *Sell car wash tickets for Phinny. Pay Macy's bill. Butter.* I found a pen and wrote the words in clear block letters. *Treasure Hunting.* I slid the notebook across the table.

My mother squinted at the page for a few seconds. "Oh! Treasure hunting!" she shouted. "I thought that's what you said."

8 - DIARY

Having hunted for my mother in her nightstand, I looked for my father under the slanted eaves of our attic, accessible from a wooden stairwell that unfolded like a trick from the second-floor ceiling. In summer the room was hot and breezeless, but in winter the cold seeped through the bare rafters, making the large triangle of unfinished space feel vibrant, alive. When I looked out one of the two tiny windows with nothing between the sky and me, I always thought of the crow that had flown off with my heart years before.

Inside the attic I loved inhaling the sweet, fragrant smell of wood as I lifted the lid on the cedar chest and rifled around for the white suit jacket my father had been married in. I slipped my arms into the roomy sleeves, feeling him wrapped around me as I turned the crisp, yellowed pages of his stamp collection book, my way of spending time with the man I wanted more than anything to love me.

My parents had met when my mother, born in 1928, was in her mid-twenties. My father, eight years older and living down the road in the shore town of Madison, Connecticut, flirted his way into a date one summer afternoon. What those early years of romance looked like require a fiction writer's imagination. Were my parents ever playful with each other? Sexy? Funny? Did they kiss for hours or only argue endlessly? Did her cigarette breath repel him back then, or did young love allow him to ignore her pack-a-day habit that would become the catalyst for nearly all of

their fights? My sassy blonde mother was a "fun-loving" major-
ette according to her college yearbook, and my father apparently
loved to dance, though I had no direct evidence of that as he
treaded heavily around the house. So how did such characteris-
tics disappear, I wondered, or at least get suppressed around our
family? How did my fox-trotting father and a vivacious gal like
my mother turn into two sourpusses with hardly a kind word for
each other—or their daughters?

I didn't have a real clue. Then, one day, I found the war trunk.

Though I had been spending time alone in the attic for years,
it wasn't until I was about ten that I first noticed the trunk shoved
into a corner. I unhinged the scratched, brass latch and opened the
wooden lid, laying bare a collection of mementos, nearly impossible to believe existed, when I had spent hours combing the house
for exactly this kind of thing. Sometimes I think the trunk just
appeared that day when I was finally ready for it, as signs often do.

That's when I heard her. "What on earth are you doing up
there, Sandy?" My mother, who detected vibrations like a snake,
must have heard me sliding boxes around.

"Nothing," I called back, already sifting through silk maps, a
doll-house-size shrine, an envelope of Japanese money curiously
marked *Pesos,* and another dozen souvenirs carried home from
World War II and stored away for decades.

I almost died twice. My father's clipped words uttered one day
while we were staking tomatoes in the garden left no room for conversation. *Japan was beautiful. Too bad I was there during the war.*

What could I say to that? Always terrified of igniting his
temper by saying the wrong thing, I swallowed back a hundred
questions.

Aware of my mother tuning in from downstairs, I quickly
dipped my hand into the trunk again, this time pulling out a
manila envelope fat with dozens of black-and-white photos. In one
my lanky young father is receiving his pilot's wings in the Army

Air Corps; in another he leans from the cockpit of a grounded plane, his narrow, brown eyes gazing into the camera. I stared at that picture, lost to something deeper than disbelief. Is this him? Is this my father smiling like that? I checked the back for names and dates.

I flipped through the stack of photos as quickly as I could, stopping at one of my father sitting on the ledge of a concrete memorial inscribed with Japanese writing. The back was marked in his handwriting: *official music of Jap Navy*. I didn't know what I was looking for, but for the first time in my life, something essential about my father became clear to me. I did not understand or relate to the brusque man who lived downstairs, but this fetching young soldier, he was mine. He lived in Japan and, like me, had collected things. We shared this.

"Sandy!"

I stuffed the photos back in the envelope then placed it carefully in the trunk. That's when I saw something else tucked into the far corner and lifted out a slender book with a blue cardboard cover: *All Services Polyglot Diary*. I drew a quick breath at my first glance of the familiar swirling script on the inside cover.

> *Property of William F. Miller 2nd Lt.*
> *Bought in Sydney, Australia, June 1945.*

When I thumbed through the book, the pages rattled like dry leaves, and the writing, all done in a consistent, blue ink pen, revealed my father's slanted script. I wanted to start reading when I heard the creak of my mother's foot on the bottom rung of the pull-down stairs. Knowing what I might be risking if caught (a spanking and banishment from the attic, death by a thousand scowls), I returned the book to the trunk and soundlessly lowered the heavy lid.

Every day for a week after that, I crept upstairs and kneeled on the raw floorboards, reading my father's war diary in the glare of a single light bulb. Because I had to strain to decipher the handwriting, only small pieces of his entries stayed with me. *Played bridge today. Went to church. Wish I had Mom's home cooking. Had a few gin slings. Raised Hell. Going to Okinawa. Hearing rumors about the end of the war. Heard from Della.*

Della? Who was Della? For weeks I wondered about that old-fashioned name. What happened to her, this Della in the diary? Did my father, as a young man, once love someone without the ties of marriage? And why didn't he marry her instead of my mother? The man in the diary felt as removed as a character in a novel, one who would cease to exist when I had turned the last page. That this twenty-five-year-old soldier was an actual person, and was related to me, seemed impossible. Still, I studied each entry, absorbing his words about war, trying to know him, this man who waited impatiently through that long, hot summer of 1945 for the Japanese to surrender. When they finally did, he wrote about his last night in Tokyo: *Ate fish. Talked with an English woman who had been interned for five years. Told us all about the Japs. Made me kind of bitter. They beheaded pilots and prayed to the winds.*

I would never forget that line. What did it mean to pray to the winds? It sounded absolutely magical, but as a Catholic girl who only prayed to God and church-approved saints, I knew it was a big sacrilegious mistake.

Finally, I read the last entry dated Sunday August 16, 1945, as he left Tokyo, flying over the Emperor's palace and Mt. Fujiyama. *The city was flattened.*

The dozens of blank pages that followed would be my father's marriage to my mother in 1954, the death of his parents, the arrival of Betsy in 1963, then my birth a year later. Another decade forward brought us to that very moment in which we all lived together in our own suburban cold war. For the first time I saw something previously invisible to me: my father as I wanted to know him when he was young and openhearted.

"What the heck have you been up to, Sandy?" my mother asked when I crawled backwards down the attic ladder that last afternoon after finishing the book.

"Just dressing up," I lied.

"Every day? Why don't you do something useful instead, like clean your room?"

"Okay, I will." I went to my bedroom that I had no intention of cleaning, locked the door, and slid a small photo out from under my shirt—my young father sitting in front of the Japanese memorial. I tucked the picture into one of my books without any concern that my mother would find it. Her expertise was in concealing things, not looking for them. Not me. I had discovered a route to connecting with my father even if he would never find out about it.

9 - CROSS

"We could just go for doughnuts," I proposed.

"And skip church?" Betsy asked.

"Who would know? God?"

"Yeah, God," she allowed, before taking a second to think about it. "But would He actually do anything about it?"

"You mean except doom us to hell?"

At seventeen years old, my sister sat tall and slender next to me on the passenger side of our blue Cutlass. We sniffed the air as we drove past a doughnut shop before pulling into a tired strip mall in downtown New Britain. Betsy hated to drive, so I, with my freshly minted license, was seated behind the wheel.

On that Sunday night, the expansive asphalt lot was nearly empty, except for a few stray cars, the majority belonging to the congregants filing into St. Mary's Church, a Catholic monstrosity of stained glass and brick. The in-between light of day and dusk was eclipsing the remaining hours of that Sunday afternoon. In the morning, another week at St. Thomas Aquinas High School would begin with the blast of our alarm clocks. Going for doughnuts, instead of to church, would add a precious hour of downtime to our overly busy weekend.

Betsy looked at me, her eyes sparkling at the possibility of doughnuts. "Wanna?"

Yes. I did wanna. That's why I said it. I wanted to go into that shop so welcoming with the smell of warm yeast and sugar, and order a pastry, then I wanted to run from that church so far and so fast, never to darken the door of it again. I wanted to flee the constraints of that factory town, quit Catholicism that mostly bored me, and escape my life in which nothing remarkable ever happened. I wanted to follow my father's diary to Japan—an idea that had been with me since I found the book years earlier. I also wanted boys to kiss, and one to love me, the way people loved each other in novels, with unbridled passion, but also real kindness. Sometimes I felt like I was propelled solely by my desire for escape, adventure, and someone who adored me. Those wants were the engine that powered me through my staid, Catholic world each day. But, at that point in my life, I couldn't surrender to any of them because I knew what the consequences would be, or, at least, Betsy did.

She was the daughter with the tidy, blue bedroom and perfect-attendance record, never missing a day of grammar school, even when running a fever. While longing led me to collect other people's discarded trash from the ground, Betsy saved her money and her Halloween candy, until she threw most of it away months later—at which point I would fish white Baby Ruth bars out of the garbage and shove them in my mouth, relishing that brief, delinquent burst of sugar. Betsy also saved Christmas presents in their original boxes, her schoolwork marked with *A's*, and me from eternal damnation when I told her that, yes, I did want to skip church.

We had both been up since 5 a.m. to work the morning shift as dietary aides at a local convalescent home and, consequently, had missed the morning service at our own parish. Since our parents' law and God's law (perhaps they shared a lawyer) required us to attend weekly Mass, our only option was a Sunday evening service at this downtown church.

Betsy would head off to college the following year. I didn't know then how fiercely I would miss her. I didn't know then that I would peer back through time, trying to salvage something of my home life from those years, and I would see us as girls bouncing gleefully on my parents' bed, pretending to fly because our mother was out grocery shopping, and this secret assault of boisterousness gave us a small taste of freedom. Only Betsy understood that the happy-family show we put on for neighbors and friends was a hoax with smoke and mirrors, much of the actual smoke coming from my mother's cigarettes that armored her behind a hazy, gray shield. Sometimes Betsy and I excavated a pack of Tareytons from her purse and either bent it in half and then returned it to her purse or dropped a few cigarettes into the toilet and let them float there, a pathetic sight for sure. But those were our small, hard-won victories against her. That was what we had together, the *us against them* that thickens the blood of siblings.

I thought about the bakery. For the fifty cents meant for the church collection plate, we could get maybe two glazed doughnuts and soon be savoring them. Yes, we'd be ashamed of our sinfulness, but at least we'd be having an adventure of sorts. And maybe for a moment I'd touch what always felt just out of reach.

But that's not what we did. Never. Rather, we slid off the bench seat of our car and crossed the street. With hands dutifully clasped in front of us, we entered the cavernous nave, dipping our fingers into the holy water and anointing ourselves with the sign of the cross. *In the name of the Father, Son, Holy Spirit, Amen.* This is what we were told to do. This is what we knew how to do and couldn't *not* do, no matter how conflicted I felt about it all.

10 · WHO

As a teenager I could always find boys, not always good ones, but they were around, patching the various potholes in my heart. But of all of those boys, I believed most ardently in the one I called *Who*.

We first met as college students at separate schools two states apart. He appeared out of nowhere with his fluffy eighties hair and almond-shaped eyes that, like mine, were always on a search. Our mutual friend Kathy had invited him down for the weekend to Drew University, our college in Madison, New Jersey, and when he wandered into my dorm room, his eyes scanned the bookshelf littered with my usual array of talismanic objects: a blue jay feather; a plastic-coated electrical wire left on a table in the Commons; a dried hydrangea flower; a turquoise Super Ball that, in lonely moments, I rubbed against my lips like a kiss. When his eyes landed on a deck of playing cards, he picked it up and shuffled with quick, sure fingers. Soon we were sitting cross-legged on my bed, drinking flat Freixenet champagne left over from a birthday party and trying to crush each other in a game of Spit.

"You're fun," he said to me as we launched into a kind of cutthroat, sudden-death round in the game that neither of us was used to losing.

He visited again, this time with his roommates, John and Jeremy, on a Saturday afternoon in early spring. Along with my friend Kathy, we squeezed into John's old Saab and drove to a wine bar in Greenwich Village.

"The Trefethen to start?" John asked, perusing a book-sized list with a soft, cordovan cover.

I looked at where John was pointing. Twenty-five dollars for one bottle? I stiffened. I had twelve bucks plus some change in my pocket. Spending it all on wine meant no laundry that week.

Did *Who* see me balking? He must have, because he touched his fingers to my forearm. "We've got this," he said. While he had my father's familiar lankiness and dark features, *Who* also had something my father never showed me—an ebullient spirit that made me feel happy.

Clustered around a table in a smoky room pulsing with the rhythm of syncopated jazz, the five of us downed the twenty-five-dollar bottle of Trefethen to start, then another. We ordered a cheese plate to share, and after we had scraped up every bit of French bread and taleggio and licked our fingers of oily black olives, *Who* leaned back in his chair against the exposed brick wall, and, as clear as a path lit by sunrise, I saw a boy who could lead me right to those hidden pieces of my heart.

On our way out, I snagged a box of matches from the hostess station and tucked it into my pocket, saving what I could of that afternoon before we all staggered, slightly buzzed, up the stairs into the dusky Manhattan night. Out on the sidewalk, *Who* pulled me to him, pressed my cheek against the shoulder of his gray herringbone coat that smelled of smoke and cold air, then he bent to kiss me.

Two weeks later on St. Patrick's Day, in his New Haven dorm room, with a tape of Keith Jarrett's *Köln Concert* setting an improvisational mood, we made love for the first time on two pushed-together dorm beds. I'd lost my virginity the year before, but not with someone I wanted to be with forever. Afterwards I scuttled naked into the cold bathroom with the chugging silver radiator. I peered at the mirror to see what love looked like on my face, elated at how being with this cute, confident boy had transformed me. For once I saw beauty, not just longing.

After that vacation, I went back to college changed. My father, I'd just learned, had colon cancer. "What does that mean?" I asked my mother. We didn't talk about bodies, certainly nothing that happened below the waist.

"He'll be fine," she assured me. "Not to worry, Sandy."

So I didn't. But if my parents had been missing from my life before, they all but vanished that semester, barely calling, occasionally sending a note with cryptic updates. *Daddy not doing so well*, my mother wrote in an Easter card sent with a chocolate bunny that I devoured in one sitting, and a lemon-yellow T-shirt that, alone in my dorm room, I tore apart at the seams. "Damn you," I shouted. "I fucking hate yellow!" *Another surgery*, my mother wrote a few days later on gilt-edged notepaper with a gold *B* embossed at the top.

Who and I wrote letters, too, on lined pages torn from spiral notebooks. We flirted in the margins and sent along photos. I would smile at the picture of him wearing only a trench coat, a strategically placed button meant to look like a penis poking out. He alone made me forget that, in the hidden background of my life, my father had cancer. *Who* helped me forget everything, and, for that reason among others, I couldn't wait to see him again at my roommate Liz's weekend-long birthday party on Long Island.

When *Who* got out of the car, I nearly dissolved into his arms. Did he detect the desperation wafting off me? Did he know I needed to escape my family, as looming loss burned like the sun that summer? I felt his reticence in the limp hug and weak kiss, in the way his eyes floated past mine. "Where should I put this?" he asked, holding up a six-pack of Molson Golden.

When we opened the first two bottles, I didn't throw out the gold caps, but kept them in my pocket, jingling them around all day like a gambling addict hedging her bets in Atlantic City.

I spent the afternoon in awareness of him, positioning myself for connection, coming to realize that he could not, would not, meet me there, or anywhere. The more he pushed me away, the more I tried to push closer. By evening, he had swapped passion for geniality, and I passed out alone that night, thoroughly wasting the lock on the door of Liz's brother's sky-blue bedroom.

When it came time to say goodbye the next day, *Who* was tossing around a Frisbee with his friend Scott, making seemingly easy banter while ignoring me, the girl in the corner of the yard—the one with a catch in her throat and tears pooled in her eyes, blinding her to everything except stinging rays of late morning sunlight.

Finally I found the courage to call out. "Hey! Can we talk for a minute?" Holding back tears felt like a job for the Hoover Dam.

"Sure." *Who* flicked the Frisbee to Scott and strode over. "What's up?"

"So, I was just kind of wondering if you wanted to have dinner together this summer, or something?"

He swallowed audibly. "I guess I should say that I'm just not good with distance. And since we're three hours apart at school, I really don't think we should get so attached."

I nodded, as if in wholehearted agreement. "Yeah," I said, "makes sense." When really the only thing I wanted in that moment was a boy, this boy, to get so attached.

A few minutes later as we drove into our separate lives, I felt the edges of the hole in my heart that had been stretched with love for the first time, and then left empty. I held tightly to my memories and two bottle caps that I later tucked in my trove in the back of my childhood closet. I had nothing more to sustain me through the ensuing months of cancer hell.

11 - END GAME

"Where do you think you're going?" my father asked as I started toward the driveway with a plan to meet my friends Diana and Marilyn for a movie. "You're not done here yet."

I was nineteen years old and home from college for the summer. Though *Who* would often occupy my thoughts as I typed and filed at the office in Hartford where Betsy and I both worked, I'd given up any hope of his resurrecting our relationship.

It was a tedious few months. Betsy and I would arrive home from work each day to a barrage of chores in a yard that was a glorious mixture of lush grass, abundant gardens, and a distinctive stand of evergreens that my father cultivated with a caring that bordered on obsession. "How about that blue spruce," he might say as he walked past it, brushing a work-roughened hand over the silvery branches. "Isn't she a beauty?"

Almost every summer evening since we were young girls, my sister and I gardened uncomplainingly until the sky and soil were the same black color. We worked on Saturday mornings, too, when neighbors would wander into the yard just to say hello, sometimes bearing a diseased plant. *I need some help here, Bill*, they would say. And my father, who not only grew up on a farm, but also worked as the Director of the Connecticut Department of Parks and Recreation, always knew what to do. *You want to cut the plant down to the main stem,* he might say. *Then sprinkle lime around the roots. It'll come back. Now, how about I buy you a beer?*

I would watch with an ache in my chest as my father and his

friend sat on our picnic table, talking easily between sips from sweaty cold cans of Schlitz. I would wonder how I could forge some connection with this man so quick to laugh with everyone else, but always able to overlook me, as if I didn't need his attention. What would it take for him to like me, too? I tried in the garden, completing each task under the auspices of my own yearning. I weeded. I planted. I watered. I dutifully built raised beds with alternating layers of mulch, manure, and grass clippings, until our backyard looked as though it were lined with rows of dirt-covered coffins. And while my father and his friend chatted, I would sneak off to a corner of the garden to pick sun-warmed cherry tomatoes. I would hold one in my mouth like a wish, then bite it slowly, savoring the seedy sweetness, trying to understand my father who could talk to anybody, it seemed, but not me.

Of course, we had some conversations, but they were typically more perfunctory than meaningful, never touching on the things I cared about. I thought often of how my father grew up with five older brothers and a three-year younger sister, Marie, whom I didn't meet until a decade after my father had died. The seven children had a stern German father and warm, but no-nonsense Slavic mother, both of whom passed away long before I was born. In adulthood, we only ever visited two of my father's brothers, which made me wonder about the disconnect fostered in his large farm family. Was that his training ground for the way he raised us—to work in focused silence? To not regard girls as worthy of his attention?

In one of the very few photos I have of us together, my father is sitting on a bench, taking a break from gardening. I am twelve years old and uncomfortably perched on the left side of his lap with my arm draped around his neck. My father's tanned arm encircles, not me, but rather our miniature Schnauzer sitting to his right. A smile plays on my lips, but it can't mask the desperation in my eyes.

That summer, when our father was too sick with cancer for physical labor, Betsy and I worked double-time, begrudgingly taking up his slack, me quietly resentful that our only interaction involved servitude and cow manure. In nineteen summers with my father, there had never been a ball toss, a bike ride, or a drive to Friendly's for an ice cream cone after hours of chores. So that night when he told me that I wasn't done yet and couldn't go to the movies with my friends, I stopped walking and turned to look at him. My father's once full, ruddy face had grown pale and gaunt. His once strapping body exposed the ravages of the failed radiation treatments. He could no longer go to work and instead rested most of the day. Still, that night, even as he stood there in what must have been excruciating pain, I selfishly felt little for him beyond resentment.

"I thought I was done," I said, each word thudding hard.

"Well, you're *not* done," he insisted. "In fact, I don't want to have to tell you what to do anymore. I want you to come to me every night and say, *Daddy, how can I help in the garden?*"

"I'm supposed to ask you that? Every night?"

"Yes. And I want you to smile when you say it, like you're pleased about it."

I swallowed audibly, trying not to fume. Then, slack-mouthed as if drunk, I asked, "Do you want me to do something else in the garden?"

Ire rose in his cheeks. "Is that how I told you to ask?"

"I don't know. Maybe."

He grabbed the top of my arm. "That's not what I said."

I tried my best to obey. I wanted to be done with my chores and flee into an air pocket of friendship. But I was born without the submissive gene. "Daddy," I finally snarled, "how do *you* want me to help in the garden?"

He raised his hand to spank me, but nearly staggered with the exertion. So instead of bringing his hand down on me, he pointed at the house. "Get in there with that attitude." He called to my mother through the open window. "Betty! Can you hear me? Teach this kid a lesson!"

My mother, her face set in a scowl, seized my arm at the door. She didn't have to know what had happened; she understood well that I needed to be set straight. When I wrested my arm away, she grabbed me again with one hand and started swatting me with the other, reaching this way and that, until she made contact with my back or butt or head. "You know what you are?" *Whack*. "You're a brat." *Whack*.

I pulled away and outran her down the torn-up hallway. As my father's health deteriorated that year, my mother had decided to redecorate the house, her way of coping with the terrible truth of his illness perhaps. The downstairs, stripped to plaster and bare wood, awaited new carpeting and wallpaper, leaving our home an empty, echoing shell. I took the uncarpeted stairs two at a time and shot into the bathroom. I slammed the door and locked it against her banging.

"Sandy! Open this door. Now! Do you hear me? Open this door!"

In the medicine chest I found my father's aspirin. I clutched the white, plastic bottle and shook it hard so she could hear. What was I thinking, that I might attempt death by an overdose of aspirin? While the idea appealed in that moment, I lacked the guts that even a half-hearted suicide attempt required. Instead I just shook those pills and dreamt of what could be: Me dead. Them pained with regret for how they had treated me.

When my mother managed to spring the lock with a bobby pin, she broke in and snatched the aspirin bottle from my hand. Then she started hitting me with it. I grabbed her hard-plastic hairbrush with the spikey bristles, and soon we were screaming and smacking and shoving each other against the Formica counter. When I finally escaped from the room, I saw my father—his eyes sunk, his chest heaving—was waiting in the hallway, his leather belt in hand.

Later that summer on the beach, I met a Southern guy I called The Cowboy. Loose-limbed and horny, we downed a six-pack in the dune grass before landing on the living room floor of my family's vacation rental. At 2 a.m. I assumed my parents to be safely asleep when, with my underwear kicked down to my ankles and The Cowboy's hands groping my hips, I startled at my father's familiar tread from the hallway into the kitchen. The Cowboy and I hurriedly disentangled from each other, grasping for our clothes, yanking up shorts in swift, quiet motion, not a second before my father peered down on us.

"Hello, Sir," The Cowboy drawled.

"Get the hell out of here," my father said, his voice a feeble rasp.

Those would be the last words he used around me for two weeks. When he did speak again, the two of us were back at home, suffering through breakfast together. In the silence made loud by the crunch of chewing cereal, my father leaned across the table and looked at me with his sharp, dark eyes. "Your body is sacred," he said. "Don't you let anyone touch it again."

My jaw set. I gathered my resolve. "Does that mean you'll stop hitting me?"

His eyes tightened, but he said nothing.

12 - MY STORY

Liz, my minister-in-training roommate, answered the 5 a.m. phone call. She climbed up the ladder to my top bunk and crawled into the bed next to me. When I realized what was happening, my heart began to beat so hard that I could feel the thudding in my throat.

It was my mother's older brother, Charlie. "Your father . . . last night . . . ."

And just like that, my entire world shifted.

I hung up the phone and lay on my back looking up at the ceiling panels, just a few feet away.

"Do you need to talk to your mother?" Liz asked gently.

"No," I whispered, shaking my head against my pillow. "She had my uncle call. I'm sure it was too much for her."

"What about Betsy?"

"I'll see her later when I go home," I said, turning to Liz, this time for guidance. If I learned anything from those first moments, it's that nothing prepares you for the day you lose your parent. No book. No independent film about grief. No late-night conversation over a passed bowl of weed or bottle of brandy. You can't possibly know that experience of having your father taken from you until it happens.

I squeezed my eyes shut, desperate for a few tears. None came. "What do I do now?" I asked Liz, my voice high and pleading. "I don't know what I'm supposed to do."

After wiping her eyes and blowing her nose, Liz suggested we make our way to the Commons for breakfast.

The cafeteria had that pungent morning smell of scrambled eggs and sausage. I self-consciously took a tray and a bowl (*Should I even be eating with a dead father?*) and ladled in a starchy lump of oatmeal. I doused it with brown sugar and milk, not sure when to stop pouring, not sure of anything as I sat down amidst the din of silverware and the clash of hard plastic plates, noticing how some things remain constant even when the foundation of your life has been altered beyond recognition. After a moment Liz joined me with her tray, then our friend Kathy, my link to *Who*.

"Do you want me to call and tell him?" Kathy asked.

"Sure," I said, as if I didn't care. But yes, I did want him to know, thinking that maybe my father's death would legitimize my desperation over the past summer.

Liz, with her warm brown eyes and explosive eighties curls, leaned in and asked, "What will you miss about your dad?"

"I don't know," I said. I thought about all the things I never had with him. Even with Liz, who knew me so well, I struggled to share what had happened—or didn't—in my childhood home. But after a moment I pulled out my two favorite memories, each the length of a blink. I'd kept them with me for years, like photos discovered after a fire had consumed the rest of the albums. I had turned them around in my head until I knew every angle and hue, until I had marked the worn surface with fingerprints and breath.

In one, my father, wearing gold swim trunks, is teaching me to body surf at Nauset Beach on Cape Cod. He is holding me in front of the approaching surge saying, "This is how you learn. Sink or swim!" I remember the terror I felt when he released me into the wave, but also the exhilaration that came with the long, satisfying ride to shore. When I staggered to my feet in the sea-foam and turned back to find my father, he was nodding his approval and signaling me out again. In my other memory, Betsy and I are bent over an apron of moss at the base of an evergreen tree in the woods on the edge of our town. My father has taken us on a nature walk, and, with his near-genius environmental IQ, is naming every flower and tree along the path. He shows us that you can identify a red pine because it has three needles on each stem, R-E-D, while a white pine has five, W-H-I-T-E. At one point he snaps a twig from a birch and holds the pale-green insides up to our noses. "How about that?" he says. When I sniff, that branch smells just like birch beer soda, so much so that I want to bite into it. In fact, I wanted to swallow up that whole day and keep it inside me forever.

He died before midnight on December 13, close to the raw, bone chill of winter. It was exam time at my college, when caffeine, sleep deprivation, and those cheap packages of instant ramen devoured in all-night study sessions had drugged me into a sluggish buzz. I had completed every paper and test, except for the dreaded statistics final still a few days away, and I needed to make arrangements to take it at home. So after breakfast, I walked to the counseling center in that disconnected state people must feel when a part of them has been hacked away, when you wake up in the hospital and learn that your leg has been amputated, but you don't remember the car accident. All you can see is incalculable loss.

Dead. Dead. Dead.

I said it over and over to myself as though I was trying to memorize a foreign vocabulary word that wouldn't stick. But no matter how many times I repeated it, anxious to wring out some meaning I could grasp, I still felt its clunky weight on my tongue. *Dead*. What did dead mean? Closed eyes? Ice-cold skin? Stiff limbs? *Dead*? Really? *Dead*?

We had spoken the day before, but I hadn't understood what he was saying.

"Hi, Sandy. It's Dad," he said, his voice a coarse whisper, "I just wanted to say goodbye."

Goodbye? Huh? He'd barely said hello, but okay. "Bye," I

told him. "I hope you're feeling okay." We spoke for another minute about school and the upcoming Christmas vacation, when I assumed I would see him. That was it. I didn't understand. Couldn't my withholding father have spelled it out a little better? *This is goodbye, as in goodbye, our final conversation on this earth. I am dying tonight. We will never talk again.*

How dare he be so circumspect, not telling me the truth in that phone call?

I would only find out later from my uncle that two hospice nurses had been coming for a week, one having mentioned the day before that the end was close. On that day, the same day he called me, my father also called four of his closest friends, not just for a phone conversation, but to invite them to his bedside. What confused me most was how *I* had not been invited? I was at school in New Jersey just a few hours away. I had a car that semester. And he didn't ask me to come. My father didn't ask me to come and see him before he died.

How does a father leave this world and not want to see his daughters? Wait. Wrong verb. How does a father leave this world and not *have* to see his daughters? As a daughter, I was outraged. Now, as a mother of two children who own the biggest pieces of my heart, I am utterly boggled. Putting the best face on it, the answer, I suppose, is that he didn't know how it would affect me, or he couldn't handle the sadness. Or, more likely, my parents decided to spare us the inconvenience in the middle of final exams. Or, the hardest possible truth of all, one that I tried to pretend away: his friends were his family, and he wasn't going to miss me all that much.

Nearly every day after that for far too many years, I would wonder how different my life could have been if, instead of a brief, disjointed phone call, I had shared an hour in that room with my dying father. What if he had said, *I need you to come?* Would his wanting me there have finally broken down our wall?

The college counselor and I sat across from each other on bland, structured furniture that made me feel as though I'd been placed in a wooden box. She was awkward in her attempt to appear relaxed and ask the appropriate questions in a thoughtful, measured tone. I was perched on the edge of the chair-box, giving short answers, eager to make a sanctioned exit. Here's what I said:

"Cancer."

"Sixty-four."

"One sister."

"Connecticut."

When really what I could have said was this: He's likely been dying for two years, but don't ask me anything about it because my parents don't really communicate with me. Even one month ago when I saw him at Thanksgiving break, it wasn't exactly cozy family times around the table.

"Daddy's in your room," my mother said when I arrived at the door with my backpack.

I trudged upstairs and paused outside my room, which had always been a place of refuge in that house. Not that night. When I peered in, I spotted the taupe levers of a hospital bed and a bag of fluid dangling from an IV stand. Then I saw him, gaunt and gray, his face sagging, his lips chalky and slightly parted. *Who is that*? I wondered. For a split second, I honestly had no idea. But then came the slow dawning. *Oh my God.* I fled across the hall and shut myself in the bathroom, where I noticed a clear plastic hospital bag, draped like an empty bladder on the towel hook. I sat on the toilet, head in my hands, sick. Without knowing how a colostomy bag worked, I understood that's what it was.

My mother pounded her fist on the bathroom door. "Did you say hello to Daddy?"

I was breathing through my mouth, willing myself not to vomit. "Not yet."

"Well get in there and say hello."

I opened the door and crept back across the hall. Trying not to inhale the thick smell of illness, I gingerly sat on the edge of the stool, the very same one I'd tipped over the night of the bakery murders as I'd waited up in fear. Here I was on that stool a decade later, with a whole new brand of terror coursing through me.

My father's eyes blinked open, then settled at a heavily drugged half-mast. It took him a long time to speak. "Hello, Sandy." His voice strained with the effort of pushing the words through his throat. He didn't move his lips when he spoke. "Give me a kiss?" He tried to grasp the sheets and pull them higher on his chest. I didn't know if I was supposed to help him or not. I didn't know anything.

I obediently leaned over and pecked at his sallow cheek then sat back down on the stool and tried to tune my voice to upbeat. "How are you?"

When he nodded, his eyes closed slowly, "Okay," he said. "I'm okay."

"That's good."

"How's school?"

"Really good."

Silence.

"So . . ." he said, prompting.

With my head low in order to avoid my father's hollow eyes, I played with my turquoise heart ring that had belonged to the child I'd been just a moment ago, before facing this adult reality of my dying father lying in my room. For the first time I wasn't afraid of him in the usual way. He couldn't hit me or hurt me as he had tried to just months earlier. But this was even more terrifying; he wanted to talk, something we'd hardly done since our argument at the end of the summer.

Looking back, I needed one thing in that moment: for him to say he was sorry, that he was wrong, that he had missed his chance to love me. But as I sat there, awkward and uncertain in the heavy silence, my fingers itched to open my closet door and shut myself inside with my trove. I was focused so hard on not crying that I forgot to breathe, and then needed to draw a deep breath that made it feel like my chest was cracking from the tightness. I needed to get through the conversation and then out the other side without suffocating in the middle.

Finally, with the courage that dying must bring, he asked, "Do you love me?"

I paused and looked past him out the dark window into the November night. *How dare you?* I wanted to shout. How dare you ignore my emotional needs for twenty years and then suddenly ask for my love? There he was, pallid and withered, and he still held the power. I wanted to tell him the truth: nothing in my life ever felt more complicated than my love for him. It was love diluted with yearning and outrage and heartbreak, a potent mixture that could not be distilled into the pure, simple thing he was asking for. Perhaps instead, he could say that he loved me. But he didn't.

"Yes," I answered weakly. "I love you."

I slipped off the stool and out the door. I escaped from the house and ran without stopping down to The Brook where I grabbed a handful of stones from the bank, then leapt from rock to rock until I reached Treasure Island. As I stood there on the granite boulder, the water forking to either side of me, I hurled the stones into the cold autumn air, feeling my pain splash and ricochet around me.

If the college counselor had asked the right questions that day, I might have told her how at Thanksgiving dinner my mother, sister, and I had sat in silence chewing our overcooked turkey breast and instant potatoes puddled with margarine while my father, too weak to join us, remained upstairs in bed. Later my mother fixed him a plate, but we didn't sit with him. That wasn't our family's way. Rather, my father ate Thanksgiving dinner alone in the hospital bed in my room while I hid on the far side of the house. When he was done, my mother sent me in for the tray. "That was good," he said, though he'd eaten almost nothing.

"Can I get you anything else?" I asked as flatly as possible. I didn't offer pie, because I didn't want to bring it to him and risk him starting another conversation about love.

"That's all for now. Thank you."

"You're welcome," I said, and hustled away.

If that counselor had asked, I might have told her how my father was beloved by his friends and the community and, until he became bedridden, went to Mass every day of the week. He could connect to God and his fellow congregants, but not to his own daughters. Our school successes went unnoticed. We went unnoticed. He seldom attended my sister's basketball games, supported my love of theater and writing, or showed a flicker of interest in us. He never saw his two daughters who were aching, I mean *aching*, for him to notice us. Worse than the violence in our house was that we were always being overlooked and silenced. "Don't ask me questions at dinner," he regularly warned us. "I'm too tired at night to talk to you."

But the violence was bad, too. When my father turned mean, he struck fast like summer thunder, until my only recourse was to hide in my closet with my boxes. I was almost ten when I started filling that Buster Brown shoebox with shells and trinkets and pennies and pebbles and matchbooks and metal pieces broken off from umbrellas.

If only the counselor had asked, *How is it to lose a father, Sandy?* I might have swallowed hard and said, *Truthfully, lady, it's fucking awful, only not for the reasons you might think.*

But I was too polite and Catholic for such an admission. Instead I said, "Thank you so much for your time. I probably should get going."

13 - DOWSED

After hours on the road in winter's early dusk, I arrived at the door of my parents' half-renovated house, which was now, in the wake of my father's death, crowded with family friends gathered in grief and support. Across the living room I spotted my mother, who was playing hostess with a cheese tray.

"Hi, Sandy!" she called. Her eyes drooped with exhaustion.

"Hi, Ma," I answered softly.

She set down the tray and worked her way over. She made an awkward effort to hug me but ended up patting my back like I was choking on a cracker. "I know, honey," she said, "I know."

But she didn't know, and I didn't either. Neither of us knew one blessed thing about what the other was experiencing through my father's death. Who was I at twenty to understand the loss of her husband, someone she had spent maybe a dozen nights apart from in thirty-two years of marriage? And she most certainly did not understand my grief for my father, who, even in death, still felt like someone to fear.

"Now, please go say hello to everyone," she said, urging me into the crowd of their friends, many brandishing cigarettes and highball glasses. They all hugged me and said the same nice things: *Your dad was the best. I'm so sorry, Sandy.* Usually I loved these people, most of whom I'd known my entire life. They were the ones my parents regularly socialized with through the Mr. & Mrs. Club at the church and, in that way, brought joy to our lives that could not be found within our family. But that night, I resented them all, for not knowing what really happened inside our house, what Betsy and I were forced to conceal for the sake of appearances, the chronic pretense of happiness required of us.

When it was time to pick up my sister at the bus station, I leapt at the chance to get out of that room, thick with smoke and grief. I drove out into the winter night, slowing the baby-blue Cutlass past St. Francis Church where my face crumpled, but I still didn't cry. Five minutes later I pulled up in front of Jimmy's Quality Smoke Shop: half porn shop, half Greyhound Bus operation. You only had to look at the place to feel like you needed a trip to confession and a hot shower.

Betsy and I hugged in the quiet darkness of the warm car and then took a good look at each other. She was one year older, five inches taller, and blonde and blue to my light brown and hazel. While Betsy had my father's height and features, and I resembled my mother, we still managed to look remarkably alike in that *you-two-must-be-sisters* way.

"Well," Betsy said, as I pulled out, "this is weird."

"Yep. How are you doing?"

"I'll be okay," she said, "How about you?" Betsy, who was studying social work at a college in Pennsylvania, had always been an expert at putting other people's feelings first. Now she was turning it into her profession and already practicing on me.

"I'm okay. Except I'm pretty sure he died in my room."

"Is that creepy for you?"

"Not really. At least he was in a hospital bed. It's gone now. Everything's gone."

She nodded. She was the only person in the world I didn't have to explain things to.

With my father's energy lingering in my room, I couldn't sleep there. Not yet. Instead I shuffled around the house, trying to settle down, first on the living room sofa, then on the carpeted floor of the den where, curled into a tight, cold ball, I slept fitfully, weaving in and out of dreams. In the early morning hours, I found myself pulling aside the drapes and gazing out through heavy eyes onto the front lawn, my thoughts fractured as I tried to grasp what this loss meant. I pictured my father's lavish gardens that would not be planted that spring. I felt the distance between us, as real as a receding tide visibly drawing away. And while scanning my memories of my father in that yard—his yard, really—I landed on a curious incident from a decade earlier when I was nine.

From behind the magenta curtains in my bedroom, I stared out the window, watching a peculiar act that, to my young eyes, looked as strange and private as sex. What exactly was my father doing out there, holding an upside-down slingshot, pacing back and forth gripping the two short ends of the Y-shaped stick like handles, while pointing the longer stem at the ground?

I finally gathered my courage to go out to the yard but stood to the side, watching with great curiosity while he continued to pace in neat rows, the upside-down slingshot seeming to yank him forward like an eager dog on a leash.

I wandered over cautiously. "What are you doing?"

"Dowsing," he answered without breaking his stride.

"What's that?"

He nodded at the stick. "It pulls when you find water."

Though watching him pace soon grew boring, something told me not to leave. Then, after a few more rows, almost like my father was trying to trick me, the stick started to tremble in his hands. In another minute, he was struggling to hold on to it.

"Did you find water?" I called.

He didn't answer as he tangled with that stick, suddenly a living thing wrenching away from him in a manner that seemed impossible. The Catholic Church taught me to believe in the transformation of the water and wine into the body and blood of

Jesus, but supernatural things did not happen in our front yard. A stick did not pull a person toward the earth, wriggling its inanimate self out of my father's grasp. Or did it? I watched as that ordinary branch drew my father closer to the ground, until he was kneeling on the grass. Finally, he dropped the stick, and without the energy of his being, the thing was no longer alive.

My father put a hand on one knee to gain enough leverage to stand, then pointed down at his feet. "That's where the water is."

"Really?"

"Yes."

"Can we dig and find it?"

"And ruin the grass? Not on your life. Now put that away," he said, wagging his finger at the forked branch. "It goes in the garage."

Three rainy winter days after my father died, my mother, sister, and I were standing in dark, formal dresses in the lobby of the funeral home when a pudgy undertaker, who looked like an overgrown frat boy in a three-piece suit, approached us. "They're preparing to close the casket," he said solemnly. Although his hands were respectfully crossed in front of him, I could easily imagine him doing beer bongs with his fraternity brothers and lighting his farts on fire. "You may go in if you wish to say a final goodbye."

I glanced at my mother. I wanted to go, but I was too embarrassed to ask. I was afraid my interest in my father's dead body would sound creepy, even voyeuristic. My hope was that she would start walking, and I'd just casually tag along.

"*I'll* go," she said.

"I can come," I offered a little too quickly perhaps, but I needed to say goodbye.

My mother stopped to look at me, just the way I feared she would—her eyes set hard in the dark, beveled rings of her exhaustion. "Now, Sandy, there's absolutely no reason for you to go in there."

"I could," I said and left it at that. I had never had a civilized conversation with her about my needs, and, with us about to throw a closed-casket funeral for my father, I didn't know how to start.

"You wait here, Sandy," she told me. "I'll be right back."

"Also," Solemn Frat Boy Undertaker said as they walked off without me, "if you would like, we can remove his wedding band. That is, of course, your decision."

"No," I said loudly enough that my mother turned sharply to look at me. "Leave the ring on him!" I pleaded.

"Now why would we do that?" my mother asked.

I didn't even know why. It's not like I had romantic illusions about my parents' marriage that transcended death and would continue for eternity in some heavenly afterlife. More likely I pictured my father's rotting bones and the decayed casket and saw this speck of gold that would linger in the earth for all time. I found something hopeful about that, knowing there would always be a piece of him left for me to find.

"I'm just going to take the ring," my mother said. Then she turned and walked toward my father, whom I would never see again.

14 - FRAME

When my sister had returned to college for her winter term, and my mother and I were left alone with a fridge full of half-eaten casseroles and a lot of unspoken grief, I phoned The Cowboy, the boy my father had caught me with on the floor of the vacation rental, and invited him to visit for a few days. If nothing else, I hoped it would fill the silence in our house.

He arrived after New Year's, and, whenever my mother ran out to the store, he and I dashed to my parents' king-size bed, where we rolled around, clothes askew, always giddy with anticipation of my mother's imminent return.

Quite remarkably, my father must never have shared the *catching-me-on-the-floor* story because my mother was perfectly lovely to my guest, to the point of trying to unload my father's clothes on him. "Now, how about this nice jacket?" she said, pressing a blue, nylon Izod into his hands. "Do you play golf?"

"No, Ma'am, I don't," The Cowboy answered. "And I'm not certain I would feel entirely comfortable wearing your (he did not say *dead,* but I could hear him thinking it) husband's clothes."

"Ma," I said sternly. "This is just weird."

"What's weird about it?" she snapped. "If they fit him, he might like them."

The Cowboy stood there, his worried hazel eyes volleying between us, trying to decide how to least offend. Finally, he draped the Izod jacket gently over the chair back, like he had been entrusted with caring for the Shroud of Turin. "If you'll excuse me, Ma'am," he said, "I'm going to use the restroom."

"Stop giving Daddy's things away," I said when The Cowboy was off hiding in the bathroom. While I was using grief sex to cope with the loss, my mother dealt by making my father disappear. He'd been dead two weeks, and she already was emptying his side of the closet into bags for the Goodwill.

"What do you care what I do with his things?"

I guess I didn't care. I only wanted the diary, but I didn't think I was ready for it, not yet. I also wasn't ready to watch my father vanish more than he already had.

Taking none of my father's clothes, The Cowboy flew home the next day. After the airport run, I went and sat in the living room where my mother, in her clipped way, was watering the houseplants.

"Will you please sit down and talk to me," I begged. I didn't know what to do with the persistent ache of sadness I felt, worsened by our once-again quiet house.

My mother set the watering can on the black stone coffee table and leaned across the couch where I was tucked into myself. I thought she was going to hug me, but instead she reached out and fluffed the three meticulously arranged pastel throw pillows. Then she stood, circled the table, and plumped the three matching pillows on the other side. Taking great care not to meet my eyes, she plucked the watering can from the table and cut back across the room.

"Please," I begged. "Sit down for one minute!" The plaster walls, still bare from the renovation, vibrated with my plea.

My mother said nothing, kept moving.

Without my father dying upstairs, I had this groundless idea that she might soften. Without his oversized personality booming into every crevice of the house, couldn't she afford to be different? Nicer? Although I'd lost my father, I thought I might get a mother out of it. But the odds were looking slim.

A sob lodged in my throat as my mother paused at the built-in bookcase next to the arched doorway. I watched as she surveyed the shelf, touching a framed photo of my sister and me as young girls and adjusting it an inch or so into a more agreeable position. I watched her figuring out, like a shadow rising out of her stick-thin body, exactly what it would take to turn around, cross that room, and sit down next to her daughter, who was drowning in grief. Then, breath held, face tight, I watched as, without a glance back, she sighed loudly and headed to the kitchen for a cigarette.

15 - SALT WATER

"Hello, is this Sandy?"

It was *Who*, the boy from college who had broken my heart that June day at Liz's party on Long Island. I was thrilled to be talking to him, hearing how he had taken a year off from his graduate program to work in New York City. I was there, too, just out of college and working as an editorial assistant at New American Library, a major publishing house in Midtown. I was also lonely, thinking often about my father who had died 18 months earlier and trying to configure plans to move to Japan.

"Scott and I have an apartment in Brooklyn," *Who* said, hesitating. "My girlfriend was supposed to come, too, but she got a job in Boston."

"And how's that long-distance thing working out?" I asked. In my desire to see him again, the girlfriend obstacle didn't discourage me, not a bit. "I believe you had a policy."

"I did. I do. Want to get together?"

We agreed to meet that evening at the subway stop near his Midwood apartment. I had been working on the reissue of Neil Simon's play *Brighton Beach Memoirs* to tie in with the upcoming movie so, beyond the romance of reconnecting with *Who*, I was thrilled to be visiting Brooklyn, the borough I'd been immersed in through my job.

As a gift to my hosts, I grabbed two books from the staff room freebie table: *How to Drive a Woman Wild in Bed* for Scott and, for *Who*, *The Joy of Cooking*.

When *Who*, still memorably lean and swarthy, picked me up at the train station, longing hit me like a blast of water from a burst pipe. "What should we do?" he asked, taking me in with his still search-y almond eyes. "Grab some dinner?"

I told him about my work project.

"Brighton Beach? Let's go," he said, as if forgetting that the last time we were together he had ignored my desire and broken my heart.

We drove through trestle-covered streets on the far tip of New York City, seeking respite from summer heat in the breezes off that lively Atlantic inlet. A patch of open sky shone like a beacon, guiding us along, until metal and brick buildings gave way to the full light of July and the sharp briny smell of the city sea. Near sunset we pulled into a small lot that served the stretch of Brooklyn's urban shoreline. Hot from baking in the city all summer and craving the salve of the ocean, it felt astonishing to be there, so far from the austerity of my attic room in the Jersey suburbs where I lived with three college friends.

"I need to swim," I said almost matter-of-factly and kicked off my ivory Payless heels that had blistered my feet to swollen redness. Without looking back, I waded into the water in my work clothes and, just like that, surrendered every stress: money, my absent mother, and the dream of moving to Japan. I still wanted to experience all of those places my father had been during the war, but I didn't know how to get there.

I pushed past to my waist in an attempt to cool the heat, until I finally sank down to my chest. When the cold entered my core, it seemed to displace the loneliness that had settled in my heart that summer. "Come in," I shouted to *Who*, fanning my arms through the saltwater, enjoying what felt like fullness.

Who peeled off his T-shirt, kicked his sneakers onto the beach, and plunged in. When he reached me, he caught me and kissed me in the faint lap of waves, my wet clothes heavy and clinging. We laughed, holding each other, and finally, swam back to the shore and fell together on the sand, where we kissed until the sky and ocean were nearly the same muted gray color, broken only by the line of lights on Breezy Point jutting into the bay. After ineffectively rinsing off, we drove back, dripping wet, to his Brooklyn apartment, leaving puddles of seawater on our trek to the bathroom.

After a shower *à deux*, *Who* and I, slightly redolent of baby shampoo, stretched a towel onto the bathroom floor and made wild, rom-com-style love in the steam.

"So, you're in New York for a year?" I asked afterward, as we lay back on the wet tiles, our bodies squished between the tub and vanity.

"That's right. What about you?"

"I don't know," I said noncommittally. "I've been thinking about moving."

"Something I said?"

I settled my head on his chest, where the thick oval patch of hair was like a throw rug. "Not this time."

"Touché."

"No. New York is just not my city," I mused, nestling into him. "I feel so small here. I can't tell if I matter." I left space for him to insert disappointment into my vaguely shaped decision to leave. But he didn't. "I've been thinking about Japan," I continued. "My dad was stationed there in World War II, and I have this idea about reconnecting with him. You know, with his spirit."

He hesitated. "Do you miss him?"

"Not in the normal way. I just hate that he's gone. Death is so final. I realize that sounds kind of obvious, but it isn't until your father dies. I miss the past with him I never had. And I miss any future chance to be close to him.

The following Friday I visited *Who* again. After riding the subway from Midtown, fretting over my clothes and hair, I staggered to his apartment door on those same cheap heels that I'd kicked off on the beach the week before. With casual urgency he led me to his bedroom, where he lit the red candle on his nicked-up night-stand, a signal I certainly didn't need; neither of us was confused about why I was there. Then, from that saggy bed, with day and night bleeding seamlessly together in summer's dusty palette, we blasted a worn tape of The Who's "It's Hard" and made loud, sweaty love.

The next morning *Who* cooked breakfast for me in his yellow kitchen with light streaming in through the large windows, light so bright that we had to squint, even indoors.

As I took my time spreading butter on a piece of toast, I could feel him leaving, not something specific he said, just a lack of ease, a distancing as his responses to my questions became increasingly more abrupt. *Sure. Yes. Uh-huh.*

I didn't understand. I wanted to shake him and say, *How can you not feel this, too?* Instead I asked, "What are you doing next Friday?"

He didn't miss a beat, like an actor waiting to recite his line. "My girlfriend is visiting from Boston."

"Oh," I said and took a long sip of coffee from a mug that I gripped as if it were an anchor, one that could keep me from sinking into myself.

I set my empty plate on the counter, then went over and sat on *Who's* lap, putting my arms around his neck. When he didn't return the gesture, I remembered the humiliation I felt as a girl when I would try to hug my father, but his arms would stay limply by his side.

That morning in Brooklyn, I didn't understand that sometimes people who we don't even realize are barriers just clear themselves from our path, plunging us ever deeper into our dark woods of searching. That morning I only knew how it hurt, like someone had picked up the butter knife and was using the blunt blade to chip out pieces off my already compromised heart.

I slid off *Who's* lap and stepped back from the cool air of his rejection. "I guess I should go to the subway," I said.

Who agreed and sketched a crude map on a paper napkin. He slid it across the kitchen table. "Here you are," he said. "This should get you there."

As I walked to the subway following my napkin map, I clenched my face to keep from crying. *How dare he*, I thought as I searched for my crow, willing her to appear, glossy black against the empty blue sky.

16 - SHATTERED

As a young girl, I broke things, delicate things that people had given to me. I smashed them on the hard surfaces of my white veneer desk and matching dresser that my mother had insisted on buying, inflicting her design choices on what should have been my space.

"Why didn't you let me pick something out?" I asked her when the truck delivered the set that looked like the furniture equivalent of Tupperware.

We had the same argument over the psychedelic rainbow wallpaper that gave me a headache (but she argued "was *very* mod"), and the magenta polyester bedspread from J. C. Penney's that I was forbidden from sitting on.

"I don't even like it," I told her when she caught me sprawled across it one day and swatted at my legs until I stood up and folded it back.

"Of course you like it," she said. "It sure cost me enough."

Knickknacks, which I really did like, became the conduit for my anger. When hatred for my mother swelled inside me like a toxic cyst that needed lancing, I'd go to the treasures—souvenirs from other people's trips that lined my bookshelves—and grab a warty ceramic frog or glass monkey from the Philadelphia Zoo, and then rap it down hard with no regard for safety. "I hate you!" I'd seethe. "I HATE YOU!" Usually a sudden sharpness would break my skin, and I'd watch the spot of blood well up on the surface in a release of pain. Just like that, my anger toward my mother would atomize.

My words couldn't touch her. My disgust had no effect. She refused conversation. But I sure could break stuff.

Only afterwards would I step back, holding my bleeding hand, and see what I'd done. Only amidst the wreckage could I mourn the loss of my porcelain Cinderella statue, or the tiny glass Eiffel Tower from my godmother's trip to Paris.

"What's going on in there?" my mother would shout, banging her palm on the door, twisting the locked knob back and forth. "Open this door right now, Sandy! Do you hear me? I said open this door!"

Frantic, I would rush to wrap my small wound in tissue and stash any broken bits of glass in the trove in my closet. Eventually I would crack open the door and she would barge in, her blue eyes lit with rage, scanning the room for signs of wrongdoing. Oddly, she never noticed the missing frog or Cinderella, but she also never noticed the blood-dotted tissue wrapped around my hand. Sometimes, days or weeks later she might ask, "Where's that horse statue that used to be on your shelf?" And I would peek in my trove to see what I had last offered to the gods of my anger, what treasure I had sacrificed to temper my pain.

Decades later, when an essay I'd written was turned into a short Hollywood film, there was a red-carpet premiere at a movie theater in Greenwich Village and a swank after-party in Soho. At one point in the evening Mark snapped a photo of Sting and me, our heads tilted toward each other, as if we were conspiring about how to arrange a ten-hour, tantric lovemaking session. When Mark and I peeked at the photo on my digital camera, we both giggled at the mysterious red glow around our heads. "*Roxanne!*" Mark crooned. "*You don't have to put on the red light!*"

When I returned home to my regular life, I had that photo printed onto a mug that I kept in my kitchen cabinet. Sometimes I would drink my coffee from it and think this is what a souvenir should be, a campy reminder of a favorite memory. Of all the souvenirs that lined my shelf as a child, almost none of them represented my own adventures like that mug did.

Then one horrid day after fighting with Mark over my continued need to flee to New York in search of treasure, that childhood urge to break something came back to me. In a house devoid of knickknacks, I reached into the cabinet for my Sting mug. The anger could not have felt more familiar, with the route to release still right there in muscle memory.

"Screw you, Mark!" I brought the mug down so hard on the counter, the handle flew off, and a white ceramic triangle chipped off the top. For one second, I felt that taproot to anger let go and a current of relief ride up my arms. In the next second, I stood in the kitchen, weeping, as that one souvenir from a magical night with my husband lay in pieces across the counter.

I had never broken one of my own treasures and, suddenly unable to bear what I had done, hurried to collect the jagged shards. As I tucked them into the trove in my closet, I realized they were horrifying reminders of how, in an instant, things, like mugs and even marriages, can be irreparably shattered.

17 - NOTHING

"Where is the stuff from the trunk?" I asked my mother. She had just returned from "a quick trip" to the mall, and I was standing in the kitchen waiting for her. "Is it upstairs?" I crossed my arms over my chest in an effort to keep from shaking. "The trunk? Where did you put it?"

It was 1987. *Who* was back with his girlfriend, and I'd left my publishing job in New York City. In an effort to save money for Japan, I was temporarily living in my mother's house.

"What trunk are you talking about, Sandy?"

"Daddy's war trunk! The chest? Is it in the attic somewhere?" I had only been home in Connecticut for two days, already disruptive to my mother's unmonitored daily routine: T.J. Maxx and Filene's Basement for white shirts and costume jewelry, then the Wawa for milk and cigarettes. While she was completing her shopping circuit that morning, I scoured the attic, turning up nothing.

"Oh, that filthy old trunk? Is that what you mean? I got rid of it." She removed a small shopping bag from her purse and squirreled it away in a cubby above the washing machine.

"So where is the stuff that was *in* the trunk?" I asked, my voice bleeding accusation. "Daddy's stuff that he brought back from Japan?'

"I think I have an envelope somewhere," she said, turning her attention to the fridge. "Would you like a grilled cheese sandwich? I'm going to make myself one. I might even put a slice of fresh tomato on it."

"An envelope?" I said, not asking how she could have crammed all of those things into a single envelope. "Can I see it?"

"Not now."

Not now was my mother's default response when I tried to press an agenda. *Not now* were words I feared more than *No*. *No* gave me something to rail against. *Not now* was me being put off indefinitely.

The next day I continued to pester my mother until she reluctantly produced a letter-sized manila envelope held closed with the clasp flattened like tiny silver wings. She dropped it on the table in front of me. On the front she had written my father's name, *William Miller*, in her looping script. I turned it over in my hands, shocked. This couldn't possibly be it. How could a trunk of photos and war memorabilia, silk maps, letters, and a book have been reduced to a nearly flat envelope? I opened the clip, expecting to at least find the longed-for diary, but when I plunged in my hand, I only pulled out photos.

"Hey! Sandy! You be careful with those! Don't just grab at them."

I shook out the envelope until it was empty. I ran my hand inside, unable to accept what I feared might be true. I glared at my mother. "Where's the diary?"

She scooted behind the gray dividing wall of the kitchen. I could hear the cellophane crumple of her cigarettes, the strike of a match, the intake of breath, and then a labored exhale.

"Where is the diary," I repeated accusingly. "Daddy's war diary. Where is it?"

"Oh. I threw that thing out."

"Threw it out?" Horror pushed my voice up an octave. "You *threw* it out?" I felt like I was watching myself in a film about a lost daughter, a dead father, and a disconnected mother who pares everyone's life down to a few photos and some meaningless salmon-colored knickknacks bought on sale at a suburban mall.

Helen Hunt plays me, and I'm trying really hard not to walk around that stupid wall and bitch slap my mother.

Though the diary was stashed away in the attic, I always felt it would be there when I needed it, pointing me toward the connection with my father that I'd been looking for my whole life. And *now* was when I needed it. I had left New York City so I could prepare to go to Japan, a journey that would offer me the chance to find, and maybe even forgive, my father. In our twenty years together, we had shared so little, but following his path was going to rectify that and maybe even give our story a different ending. But I needed the diary to do it, to trace his path, to take him with me.

Seconds later I smelled the nauseating drift of cigarette smoke.

"Who the hell would throw out a diary?" I shouted.

"You watch your language, missy!"

I smacked my hand against my forehead and screamed. "Who the *heck* would throw out a diary?"

"I did. That's who. It was full of fish moths."

"Fish moths? What in God's name are fish moths?"

"Oh, you know, silver fish. Whatever you want to call them, those awful creatures that get into books. It's practically impossible to get rid of them. I had to throw it out or we'd have an infestation."

"Seriously? You were afraid of an *infestation* of fish moths?"

"That is exactly what I was afraid of!"

"Tell me this is a joke? Please?" I started to cry, the tears just fell without me bothering to wipe them away. "Tell me that you did not throw out Daddy's diary!" My father had done many callous things when he was alive, but my mother's latest act felt incontrovertibly cruel. I had waited for years to see that book again, too afraid of my father's wrath to risk rereading it when he was alive.

"I don't know what you're making such a big fuss about," my mother said. "It was a *book*."

"It was . . . it was . . . Daddy's diary," I sputtered. My breath left my chest, and the blood seemed to drain from my legs. I collapsed in the nearest chair.

"It was *Daddy's* diary," she mocked. "Does everything have to be such a big stinkin' production with you, Sandy? Does it? Huh? Does it?"

I picked up the photos and slammed them on the kitchen table with no satisfying effect. I made a fist and pounded it down exactly as my father used to do, causing the clock radio from Caldor's to skitter and the yellow vase of chrysanthemums to topple over, splashing stale water down the wallpaper and onto the floor. I picked up the vase and was ready to smash it down on the linoleum when my mother, eyes blazing, appeared from behind her wall. She grabbed the vase from my hand and shoved past me to kneel down in front of the puddle of water. "Now look what you've done! Cripes. You ruin everything, Sandy. You really do ruin everything!"

18 - WHY

After one week of living with my mother in New Britain, we had moved past the fish-moth debacle as we moved past everything: by pretending it had never occurred.

While my mother, in her characteristic way, developed amnesia about my father's diary, I, conversely, would toss in bed at night, warming my pink polyester sheets with worry as I wondered how I would get to Japan. That book was supposed to be my Baedeker, my huggy, *and* my father's companionship, all held between two blue cardboard covers. But it was gone, and so were many nights of sleep lost to mourning it. Without a workable plan for Japan, I accepted a job as a receptionist at the local YMCA, answering the phone and taking applications for gym memberships.

The first few days passed uneventfully, but then, on my third afternoon, I saw him. He had a runner's build and dark brown hair brushed back from his high forehead.

"I'm Jack, a long-time member," he said, approaching me with his hand outstretched. "You must be the new receptionist." Up close, I saw the fine web of wrinkles around his eyes and realized he probably had a decade on me. He also had a wedding band. Still, as I went to shake his hand, my body stretched toward him.

Meanwhile, in what could have been a tedious workday with a brown-bag lunch prepared by my mother as the one high point, my awareness that Jack would be strolling through those doors each afternoon thumped like an arrhythmia in my heart. When I couldn't find my unavailable father, I found a different tall, dark, unavailable man. Maybe that was too easy, or maybe that's just how some attractions work; we greedily seize what is there in the absence of what is not.

Each day he would stop to say hello, leaning across the front desk, resting on a tanned arm, never mentioning his wife, always probingly curious about me. "How are you today, Sandy?" he would ask just a tad too flirtatiously. Each day, he stayed a little longer, asked a few more questions about the publishing job I'd left in New York, or my plans for the evening. And I would poke at the possibility, the way you might stir a stick through a struggling fire, teasing the sparks, knowing you have the power to create that first lick of flames or let the embers go cold. I chose the flames, and one Sunday after church we met, ostensibly to go for a run. Instead we went to the Grantmoor Motor Lodge on the Berlin Turnpike, where about 38 bucks bought you a four-hour short stay. Jack went in and paid cash at the desk while I waited in the car. Then we drove around the parking lot to our room in the back and ducked inside like the cheaters we were.

Later that night I lay awake in my bedroom. With the renovation finished, the four upstairs rooms had been wallpapered and carpeted in shades of pink, the color of cooked shrimp. "It's not shrimp. It's salmon," my mother insisted.

"Great," Betsy said when I reported the conversation to her on the phone. "Our bedrooms have been salmon-ized."

Salmon or shrimp, our house felt sterile. With everything changed, discarded, or reupholstered, I couldn't find my father anywhere, and whether my mother intentionally made him disappear or not, didn't matter. The thing is, he was gone. The trunk was gone. The diary was gone. Everything was gone except one photo of him in the living room, a pleasant, smiling face, like an actor's headshot cropped into a pale-pink ceramic frame. Every time I passed it, I wanted to pick up that frame and smash it against the wall, shattering the lie of serenity it told. "That's not him," I wanted to shout. "That's not my father!"

Lying in bed thinking about my life, I felt both younger and older at the same time. Living in my mother's house, sleeping in my childhood bed made me feel like a kid who couldn't grow up. But having sex in a sleazy motel with a married man made me feel decades older than I actually was. In other words, lost in time.

I needed to move on, but where to? Where was I supposed to go?

19 - BERM

"So why did all of those clues fit Floyd Bennett Field so well?" I asked David.

It was March 2012, and I had ducked out of my life to go on a third treasure-hunting trip to Brooklyn, this time with Mark's blessing, or more accurately, his desire for respite from my insufferable moodiness. "Go," he said, like he was shooing me away. "Do whatever it takes to make yourself less miserable."

If I wasn't exactly miserable, I was in a state of misery. After spending one day most weekends sitting at Pizza World with a basket of stale rolls and forty-seven years of distance between my mother and me, I would return home empty and irritable.

"Some of the clues still fit," David assured me, "but I don't think we had the right crow's nest. This area works better in every way." Suddenly our year-ago failure at Floyd Bennett Field faded to distant memory. We were poised, at last, to find that gold in the Park Slope neighborhood around Prospect Park, just a spit from Midwood where I had spent those long-ago summer nights with *Who*.

David was somehow convinced we had to shift our focus to this fashionable area with the imposing, nearby Williamsburg Savings Bank Tower as our new and improved crow's nest, and I didn't object. I had learned plenty about treasure hunting from him, not least of which was how, just like in life, getting attached to the incorrect path can force you off track. Sometimes you have to acknowledge the errors of your ways and move on.

Since David had explored Park Slope the summer before while

on his way to a Jersey Shore vacation with his family, he cruised effortlessly through the congested streets before gliding into a parking spot near our targeted digging location. In contrast to his Brooklyn ease, I felt like a stranger in the strange land of New York City, a place that never became mine, despite the year after college I spent working here. I never felt tall enough, sexy enough, posh enough, or cool enough for this place. Once while I was studying a foldout pocket map in a Greenwich Village coffee shop, the waitress rather candidly asked if I had ever noticed how the five boroughs resembled male sex organs. "See that," she said, pointing at an uncircumcised Manhattan hanging down in the middle. "If that doesn't look like a big old cock, then I'm a lesbian or something." Stunned, I saw her point. New York City was *so* boy. And every time I went to embrace him, I felt rebuffed, as if by a lover that wouldn't have me, as if by *Who*.

As always with our digs, I followed David's confident lead, this time into a narrow area of trees and shrubbery dividing Flatbush Avenue and Plaza Street. With new spring growth still filling in, anyone on the street could see David stumbling along with a metal detector and empty ten-gallon kitty-litter bucket for lugging out the gold when we found it. A few steps behind, I was toting the shovel, trowel, and our bagged lunches. As we pushed forward another fifty feet across the top of the berm, an airplane roared promisingly overhead.

"Look for the flying birdie," David said, quoting the video in his best pirate growl. "Follow his path, but away from his nest."

"So we're right under the flight path!" I said. "And LaGuardia Airport is definitely our flying birdie?"

"Final answer," David said. "Argh!"

"Let's dig," I said. "Argh!"

Minutes later, there we were at midday, in plain view of all passersby, metal-detecting in a public space that cut through one of the most well-trafficked areas in Brooklyn. While no one looked at us suspiciously—heck, no one looked at us—I had to wonder what kind of attention we'd be getting if we were *burying* something instead of digging it up.

"This feels just a little flawed," I finally admitted to David, trying to sift out any hint of accusation. "How could someone get a giant chest in here without being seen? Wouldn't they be stopped or followed?"

"But the clues fit," David insisted, "and that's all we have to go on. Clues."

"You're such a scientist about this."

"Well, that's how this kind of treasure hunting works. It's systematic."

"But that doesn't answer my question," I pressed. "How could two people sneak in here with a huge treasure chest and not have someone come in and dig it right back up—or call the police, or the bomb squad?"

"Maybe they buried it at night."

I lowered my head and looked up at him with raised eyebrows. "In the city that never sleeps, you mean?"

"But the clues fit."

While I wasn't convinced David was right, I didn't know how to assert myself around him. It was a two-part problem. First of all, he'd done the bulk of the code cracking to get us here, while I had played the supporting role of sounding board and pirate cheerleader. Without an alternative solution, I had nothing to suggest. Second, it was that *Man*-hattan thing. David was a big, tall, smart man like my father, so I was afraid to argue too vociferously. Unlike with my father, I wasn't worried David would hurt me in any way, but he might not invite me along anymore. More than I needed to be right, I needed to go on those treasure hunts, which meant I was back to following David's quite possibly flawed plan.

Using Google Earth, he had mapped out 250-feet from a ship monument, sparing us the need to measure that distance with a string as we had before. That's where we—well, he—expected to find the chest. But after smacking our shovel into resistant tree roots for the better part of two hours, we didn't turn up much beyond some rusty soda cans.

"Are you worried that we haven't found anything yet?" I asked.

"Of course I'm worried," he snapped. "What do you think?"

David was seated on the upside-down kitty-litter bucket devouring some tempeh concoction that looked rather like the damp log I was leaning against. Vegan since age twenty-two (when he received a fellowship to study vegetarianism in Europe), he could be sanctimonious about his dietary choices, holding out enough quiet judgment that I couldn't enjoy a turkey and cheese sandwich in front of him. For that reason alone, I was scooping up lumps of hummus with baby carrots while craving some animal byproduct that would put a dent in my hunger.

We made almost no conversation at lunch, except when David shaded his eyes and squinted at yet another airplane that flew overhead in a roaring taunt. "Damn flying birdies!" He drew a long breath and then exhaled loudly through his nose. "What are we doing wrong?" he asked out loud.

I didn't say it because I had no rational basis for my knowledge, but the answer was "something." We were doing something wrong. I knew intuitively from all the wrong turns I'd made in life, when I ended up in the wrong job or the wrong bed. I didn't always know right, but I sure could recognize wrong. And maybe it was time, I thought, to start asserting myself a bit more in this treasure hunt. If David's plan felt *wrong*, wasn't it up to me to find *right*?

After lunch, leaving David alone to dig, I wandered to another berm on the opposite side of the plaza. I walked into the center, sat down in the dirt, and drew my legs against my torso.

Beyond the nonexistent treasure chest, it had been a tough stretch at home. I'd been going to visit my mother one day each weekend, coming back empty, depleted, and taking it out on my kids, mostly Phinny, whose laidback style often clashed with my own more controlling ways. I figured if I didn't micromanage their lives now and then, they'd end up adrift. Wasn't it my job to keep my children from failing in this increasingly cutthroat world?

"What the hell do you want from me?" Phinny had asked the night before as I was preparing for my trip to Brooklyn while simultaneously bossing him around.

"For starters, I want you to stop using a swear word in every sentence." I pulled my backpack from my closet and searched around for my beat-up sneakers. "And I want you to work harder in school, help more at home, and just do your best at all times."

"I'm doing my best!" He stormed into his room and slammed the door in our great family tradition.

"Well it's a pretty weak best," I shouted at the closed door. "So try to do better!"

"Fuck you!" Phinny shouted.

"I think it's good you're going away tomorrow," Mark said when, a few minutes later, I joined him downstairs in the kitchen. I didn't even wait for him to leave the room before tearing open the bag of chocolate chips and cramming a handful in my mouth. "You guys need a break from each other."

"This isn't for you to figure out," I said. "It has to do with Phinny and me."

"Well Phinny is fine, and you need to lay off him."

"He's not fine."

"He's fine. He's better than fine. He's great."

"Perhaps you're the one with the problem then," I said, immediately regretting my words that filled the air around us like dark smoke.

"Just go to New York," he said. "I hope it gives you what you need. Because I don't know what that is anymore."

What should I have said? *I'm scared. I'm lonely. Watching my mother grow weaker feels like it's stripping me of my strength, too.*

Yeah. I probably should have said something like that, but I didn't. Instead I wolfed down half the bag of chocolate chips as I packed the next day's lunch of carrots and hummus.

At five o'clock, I found David, who was doing the same thing I had been doing across the street, except that hundreds of commuters filing past could see him sitting there propped against the base of a tree.

"Nothing?" I asked.

He shook his head.

I looked around wondering what we had missed. Why did success suddenly feel elusive, impossible even? Though Brooklyn was only four hours from Boston, it took so much arranging to get there, and always at some cost to my relationship with Mark. Since becoming a parent, nothing felt easy, at least nothing that I needed for myself. I had always wanted children, without fully grasping the toll it would take on my creative life. I never expected that my worry for them would fill every one of my cells like breath. I pulled out my phone and texted Phinny: *I love you.* A moment later he wrote back, *I love you, Mom.* Man, oh man, that kid had a forgiving heart.

I turned to David. "I've been starving since lunch," I said. "Can we please go get something to eat?"

Over vegetable curry we explicitly avoided talking about the treasure. The wound of not finding it again was too raw for both of us, and we'd soon be returning home, relaying another pathetic chapter in our failed treasure-hunting tale. I was beginning to feel like the girl who cries gold, and, understandably, my children's interest in my adventure had waned. They no longer peppered me with questions, as they had so eagerly in the beginning.

"How do you do it?" I asked David halfway through dinner. Of his three daughters, two had diabetes, requiring him to wake up several times a night and check their insulin levels. "How do you have your career and be a single dad with full custody and still go treasure hunting without feeling guilty?"

"Oh, I feel guilty," he said. "I don't have enough time right now to do this, but it's also my escape."

"Do you worry about your daughters?"

He looked at me, his brow furrowed, his mouth open in astonishment, like I was his mute friend who had just spoken her very first word ever. "You're serious?"

"Yeah," I said.

"I worry all the time." He stabbed a green bean and chewed it slowly. "Yep. All the time."

"Is that why you go on these treasure hunts?" I asked.

He laughed and dove his fork into his food again. "What do you mean?"

I wanted to know what made David want to dig. Did loneliness motivate him, too? What was he looking for beyond the chest of gold? "Why are you here?"

"I'm starting to wonder that myself. I can't do this again without at least ninety-nine percent certainty. I don't have the time to invest in another trip."

"Okay, but why are you really here?"

The muscles in his face tightened and then loosened before finding a resting spot, the way an autofocus lens on a camera adjusts. "Because I want the money to take Jenna and the girls on a vacation," he began. "Because I love treasure. I'm good with clues, I guess."

"So you're telling me it doesn't have to do with being an only child and your parents divorcing when you were a kid? Your own ugly divorce? Getting away from your family for an adventure? None of that?"

He looked at me, another bean poised thoughtfully in front of his mouth. "Yeah. Probably that, too."

20 - FAITHLESS

Ten weeks after giving birth to my son, I had an emergency appendectomy. When I needed help, my mother agreed to come up from Connecticut for a few days. Though a kitchen wiz in her own home, she suddenly struggled to fix me a cup of tea or heat a can of chicken noodle soup, leaving me to direct her through the cottony haze of my Percocet high while Phinny squirmed in my arms.

"Won't it be wonderful having a baby around at Christmas?" I asked my mother. I pressed my nose against Phinny's warm head. His scalp smelled creamy and a little sour, like buttermilk.

Without looking at me, my mother set her hands down on the counter and pursed her lips. "No, Sandy. It won't."

My head snapped up. "What?"

She grabbed the sponge from the sink and wrung it hard. "It would be wonderful to have a *baptized* baby around at Christmas."

I felt the choke in my throat. My tears fell onto Phinny's fuzzy brown hair. When he began to shift again, I held him so tightly that my abdomen pulsed. I didn't know yet that I had developed a severe infection following the surgery. I'd hardly eaten. I was trying to wean myself off pain medicine and get back to nursing, but then her words, as sharp as a scalpel, reopened the wound that I had wrongly imagined this baby boy, her first grandchild, had the power to heal.

I tried to argue, willing my thick tongue to lash back, but nothing came out. Really, there was nothing to say, or nothing else

I needed to hear. What she had said explained her sullenness and distance since arriving the previous day.

We were well past the time of a traditional baptism with Phinny, and our plan to do a spiritually all-inclusive ceremony at the beach on his first birthday just wasn't going to cut it with her. But did she have to reject him, her grandchild? He never asked to have lapsed Catholic parents like Mark and me.

"Go!" I heard myself tell her through the fog of drugs. "I don't want you here anymore." My mouth pulled back, and I winced. All at once I hurt everywhere. "Mark can put you on the next bus."

"Fine, Sandy. If that's what you want." She slapped down the sponge and stormed off to the guest room to pack her bag.

"It's not what I want," I called after her, my voice too weak to reach her bad ears. "I want you to love us no matter what." As I heard the door slam shut, I wanted to curl into myself and sob, but I had my son in my arms and couldn't. I did everything for my boy, so why couldn't she do this one thing for me: be a mother.

Even after a doctor treated my infection and the wound scarred over, I would wake up at night for months, casting off the comforter and then drawing it tightly around me again. I would cocoon myself and then kick to get free, as if I couldn't decide what I needed: closeness or release. My mother's words tormented me and made me sleepless with frustration and fury as I revisited the ongoing saga of how Catholicism had wedged its way between us, divesting me of both my faith in the church and my mother's unconditional acceptance.

I was eighteen and in my second week of college the day that I fully rejected Catholicism. Guided by habit and obligation, I had gone to Mass at the university chapel the first week, but the following Sunday evening, as I was squeezing into my good jeans, that proverbial lightning bolt of awareness struck. I flopped down on my bed and let out a deep breath, as if exhaling a lifetime of confusion. Three states away from my parents, I did not have to spend an hour proclaiming my faith "in one holy catholic and apostolic church," as the prayer went. And they would never know.

Looking back, I'd never been able to reconcile the violence in my home with the teachings of a church that preached kindness and turning the other cheek. At Mass each week, we were the lovely Miller family with our hands clasped in prayer, our heads bent in pious devotion; back at home in the afternoon, we practiced blistering cruelty. Church offered me an hour of respite from the coldness of my home, but it was also a place where I had to pretend that we really were a happy family. That Sunday evening in my dorm room, I was done participating in what felt like my parents' game of make-believe. I peeled off my good jeans and flicked on the television. And, just like that, the blanket of faith I'd been clumsily knitting for eighteen years unraveled in my lap.

It was one of the most liberating moments in my life, but also one with the most devastating of consequences.

≈

"What is your priest like?" were my father's first words when I arrived home for Thanksgiving break my first year. "Nice guy?"

"Father Joe?" I asked casually while bolting toward the stairs to avoid a full interrogation. "Yeah, he's great."

My father died before he learned that I'd left his faith. My mother, however, fully understood that I'd rejected Catholicism when Mark and I didn't have a church wedding. "Since it's not a real wedding," she told me a week before the ceremony, "I'm just going to wear a pantsuit instead of a dress." When Reverend Liz, my college roommate, led Phinny's "Welcome to the World" ceremony on a Rhode Island beach, my mother, who was vacationing with friends a short ferryboat ride away, refused to attend. "Is it that important, Sandy? It's not a real baptism."

I never considered the extent of my mother's pain, that by for-saking her God and breaking the chain of Catholic sacraments, I had spurned her. Would our adult relationship have developed dif-ferently if I had grown up to be the God-fearing adult she wanted me to be? I'm not sure I ever would have gained her full respect, nor would she have gained mine, but at least our mutual reverence for the church might have bound us together, the way it seems to have done for many other families I've known. As it was, the unraveling of my faith had taken with it an opportunity to reclaim something I'd always hoped had been there, but maybe never was.

When I was living in my mother's house and working at the YMCA, I kept up the Catholic ruse by attending Mass with her. Later, on Sunday afternoon I would have hurried sex with married Jack in the back seat of his car or in a hotel on the Turnpike. Unlike the ritual of transubstantiation, that most reverent moment in the Mass when the bread and wine became the body and blood of Christ, our connection of real flesh—hot, alive, and forbidden—provoked something divine in me. Bereft of my father's diary and an accessible version of my mother's love, I turned to the back seat of a two-door Chevy; it was a makeshift chapel of redemption where my breathy prayers of longing briefly felt heard.

21 - SIGNS

"You're living here in New Britain and having an affair with a married guy?" Paul snorted. "Wow. What a life." In for a week from California, Paul was hunched over an orange table at Arby's, inhaling his roast beef sandwich. "That's so pathetic."

"Shut up!" I said.

Tall and broad-shouldered, with a swagger that read gay (in time, this would reveal itself to be an accurate reading), Paul was my oldest childhood friend, and maybe because we had such a history, he never censored himself with me.

"You can't stay here anymore," he chided. "I won't let you."

"I'm still figuring out the whole Japan thing," I told him. "My mother messed everything up by throwing out that diary."

"Forget the stupid diary. Just come to Los Angeles. I work with this musician, Stefan, who has an unbelievable loft downtown. He needs a roommate. You can move in with him."

I sat back in my chair but felt my heart lurch forward. I never ignored an instinct from the gut, or the heart. Perhaps I was ready to move on. Wasn't I just biding my time, waiting to make a plan for Japan? A professor at my college had recently recommended me for a teaching job at a Tokyo university, but I wouldn't have an answer for several months. In the meantime, I didn't have the diary. I had no real interest in being with a married man, not to mention that the guilt tormented me. And my mother and father were nowhere to be found. I looked at Paul. "Fine," I said. "I'll move to LA."

Two weeks later I was gazing down on the City of Angels where the lights below glowed with startling vigor, as if Christmas had spilled out everywhere. I could always anticipate the sensory experience of New York City—the charred smell of roasted peanuts, the assault of noise and neon in Times Square, the dissonant symphony of taxi horns, and buildings that pulled your eyes up into forever. New York was tall, elegant, crowded, and villainously arrogant. That night I saw Los Angeles as it would always appear to me: sprawling and luminous with an endless vista of undimmable lights.

Paul met me at the airport and drove me to the apartment building, which he had neglected to mention was just a block from Skid Row in the sketchiest part of downtown. Shattered bottles formed mosaics of glass on the streets, and a haze the color of dirty dishwater hung damply in the night air. "I don't know, Paul," I said, looking out the car window. "This doesn't seem, um, safe."

"Well, too late," he said cheerfully. "You live here now."

Inside told a different story. The Santa Fe Artists Building had twelve floors of industrial lofts, a spare foyer with a freight elevator, and the funky vibe of working artists and musicians. The apartment itself looked like a movie set with eighteen-foot ceilings, two walls of six-foot windows, and 2,000 open square feet of floor space.

The next afternoon I was scanning the want ads in the *Los Angeles Times* when my new roommate burst through the door.

"Hey, you must be Sandy!" He held out his hand and shook mine so forcefully I had to stand up to keep my wrist from snapping. "I've got to go unpack my truck out front. I could use some help." Stefan had curly black hair cropped close to his head and skin the color of cocoa powder. Although he probably had an average build, he felt tall and, with his wide feet pointing out in first position, he moved like a determined duck.

As I helped him unpack his musical equipment from a

weekend gig in San Francisco, he told me about himself, how his mom lived up in the Bay Area and his biological dad, who was African-American, had left for good when Stefan was just a baby. He did data entry for the Skid Row self-help agency where my friend Paul also worked. The part-time job left him time to build his music career.

"It's hard in LA," he told me, as he held the elevator door open so I could carry out his guitar while he wrestled with a speaker. "It's easier to play in San Francisco. You should come with me sometime."

"Sure," I said. "That'd be great."

He propped our loft door open with the speaker and darted back to the elevator for the second one. "Ever been to San Francisco?"

"Actually, this is my first time in California."

Stefan stopped what he was doing and stood to look at me, hands low on his hips. "Why are you here again?"

I stood there carefully holding his guitar. "I'm trying to figure out how to get to Japan."

"Well, you're halfway there now," he said. I studied the deep groove in his top lip, and his eyes, dark brown and full of life. His voice made him sound enviably certain about everything. When we were done, he took me up to the roof of our building, a flat, open expanse twelve floors above the city that was suddenly my home. I sat on the low cement wall and peered over the edge where even Skid Row looked like a stage set for the players who staggered about slurring their monologues and gesticulating wildly.

"Downtown's gone from bad to worse in the time I've lived here," Stefan said. "See that burned-down movie theater?" He pointed across the street at a shell of a building with the remains of a marquee. ERT RO A I ER. I loved how it read like a code. "When I moved in, that sign said ROBERT DENIRO TAXI DRIVER, but about a month later the theater was gutted by fire. For a long time, it said BERT NERO TAX DRIVE like he was running some kind of fundraising operation. Then it said BERT RO AX RIVE, also great. Now this. Primitive sounds."

Or a puzzle falling apart, I thought.

"Is he cute?" Liz asked later that night when she called to check in.

"Sexy in an unexpected way," I said. "You know that kind that sneaks up on you? But he's not my type. Not at all."

"Hmm."

"Hmm what?"

"Just hmm."

22 - HOLLYWOOD

As Liz's prescient *hmm* suggested, soon I was dating Stefan, making weekend trips with him to his gigs in San Francisco and vanquishing the loneliness I'd carried with me like an extra suitcase from the East Coast.

I scored a job editing manuscripts for a West Hollywood literary agent named Sherry, who had an explosive personality and magnificent bosom that she would press hard against your body when she hugged you, something she did with nearly everyone she met. In contrast to the sometimes haughty corporate culture of New York publishing, Sherry had a rather different idea about work. Her core values distilled down to this: *Let's make money and have fun!* Every moment spent in that sunny LA office was an adventure in lunches, hard work, hugs, and gossip about the stars she had kissed, or wanted to. We edited manuscripts and planned book deals, took meetings at the Warner Bros. lot and pored over contracts. Sometimes, weary of the quotidian workings of the publishing world, Sherry would call "Girl's Day!" and, despite my protests that I had too much editing, off we would go in search of cute tops and highlights.

"I think you should be at every meeting I take, honey," Sherry told me on one of our Girl's Days, as we reclined in salon chairs and let the flamboyantly gay hairdresser, whose *Star Cutz* book we were hoping to represent, make me dirty blonde and turn Sherry ever more platinum, not unlike my mother's trademark do.

"You're my assistant. No. No. No. You're my associate. That sounds classier."

The next day she ordered business cards with my name embossed in gold—*Sandra A. Miller, Associate Agent*—and boasted to our clients how I had been an editor in New York City, as if this were a carefully executed career move and not a lucky landing.

In time, with the help of those highlights and some trendy clothes from Melrose Ave. boutiques, I shed my closet of New York black for the bejeweled styles of the West Coast in the late eighties. Soon I started looking the part of a California literary agent who lived in a downtown loft with her musician boyfriend and dined with celebrity clients, Betty White among them.

The night I joined Sherry and Betty for dinner at Martino's Ristorante, I wanted to tell the beloved actress how faithfully I had watched *The Mary Tyler Moore Show* growing up, and that I dreamed of becoming some version of Mary with my own apartment, a job in a newsroom, and dates with droll men in Nero suits. But I didn't mention any of that to Betty White. In 1988 when we chatted over plates of pasta and white wine, she was a *Golden Girl* who oozed grandmotherly warmth as she rhapsodized about puppies and her *Pet Love* books that Sherry represented. I had an awful cold that night, so Betty worried over me, pulling a tissue from her bag and pressing it into my hand. "Here you go, dear," she said. "You sound miserable." Instead of using the tissue, I went to the bathroom and blew my nose on toilet paper. Later I put Betty White's tissue in the trove in my top dresser drawer, since I didn't have a closet in Los Angeles.

"How's it going in LA?" my mother asked on one of our monthly phone calls. "Meeting any Hollywood stars?"

I filled her in on my dinner with Betty as well as my tedious conversations with Sylvester Stallone's mother, Jackie, who regularly dropped by the office to work on her astrology book that Sherry had sold. "She doesn't shut up," I said. "You would think it would be fun to hear her complain about Brigitte Nielson taking advantage of poor Sylvester, but not really."

"Is that right, Sandy? Sylvester Stallone? You sound like *People Magazine*."

"Oh, and my roommate is friends with Prince Albert of Monaco from their acapella group in college," I went on. I could tell that I had her full attention. These were the kinds of superficial, glitzy things we could talk about. "We all went out to dinner a few times when he was in LA."

"Well how about that? Prince Albert! Was he in a can?"

"He was," I said, laughing, "but somebody let him out."

"Well that's good, Sandy. Now why don't you get a date with him? Maybe you could be a princess instead of . . ."

"Instead of what?"

"Instead of going with that roommate of yours."

I paused. "What are you talking about?" For all of the dating I had done, I hid every relationship joy and pain from my mother. Like the treasures I kept secret, I never used the words *love*, *boyfriend*, *sex*, or *breakup* in reference to my personal life with her for fear of how callously she'd treat matters of my heart. She had met *Who*, and some college guys that visited me over summers, but there had never been a conversation about what any of them meant to me. I could not allow myself to be that exposed to her scorching criticism.

"Paul's mother showed me some pictures he sent of all of you at some party," my mother said. "I'm just suggesting that maybe you could date Prince Albert instead."

"Instead of a black guy? A musician? What are you saying?" My chest tightened. We were 3,000 miles apart, but the space between us felt like a fault line, a concealed weakness that, at any point, could trigger a perilous earthquake of unchecked emotion.

"Just forget it, Sandy. You misunderstand everything."

"No, I don't," I retorted. "I'm actually trying to understand what you're talking about. You find out that I have a boyfriend, but instead of asking me something about him, you suggest that I shouldn't be with him?"

"I'm joking. You can't even take a joke."

"It's not funny," I told her, before hanging up. "Your judgment of me has *never* been funny.

One night in LA, I got off the bus from work and headed toward my apartment building when an emaciated black woman who moved like a giraffe—long torso leaning forward, legs bowed in an exaggerated way—ambled up beside me. "Nice little girl like you shouldn't be hanging around here at night," she said. "You crazy or something?"

"I live downtown," I told her. "In a loft on Sixth."

"While I'm Tai Tai, and I'm bringing you home." Tai Tai, clearly a heroin addict and likely a prostitute, too, escorted me through the dark streets, striding uneasily on her skinny legs.

When we arrived at my door I reached into my wallet and offered her a dollar. "Thank you," I said.

"Anytime. Tai Tai's here for you. Can't be having little girls like you just walkin' around here alone. You only got a buck?"

I dug around until I found another single. "Aren't you nice?" she said and plucked the bills from my fingers.

Tai Tai and I became buddies of sorts. If she happened to be at the bus stop when I was getting off, sure enough she'd call out to me. "Sharon!" or "Over here, baby!" She would walk me to my door, making small talk along the way. "Books? Seriously? You write books? Like real books? You must be smart."

"Not write," I corrected. "I'm an agent. Writers come to me, and I try and *sell* their books to editors."

"Still. Books. That's cool. I like books. I don't have any, but I like them."

The next time I saw Tai Tai, I handed her a signed hardcover copy of *Dreamgirl: My Life as a Supreme* by Sherry's client Mary Wilson. Sherry had three copies and never missed what I took from the office and added to my own broken box: her candid photos of celebrities, buttons from book promotions, jewelry, scarves, lipsticks, postcards, and letters from ex-lovers who would find her again when they passed through town. Our office was a jumbled treasure chest of Sherry's feminine frivolity, and I regularly helped myself to what she cast off, not unlike the way I dug through my mother's nightstand drawer. The difference being that I *understood* Sherry, and in that way, she became a surrogate mother—warm, outrageous, open, and kind.

"You brought this for me?" Tai Tai asked, hugging the hardcover Mary Wilson book to her concave chest. "You know her?"

"I met her quickly when she came by the office."

"Really?" Tai Tai punched my arm. "Shit! I can't believe this."

Once inside, I would ride the freight elevator to the fourth floor, where Stefan, with his erratic schedule, might or might not be there. On the rare evenings that he was kicking around the loft, filling it with his restless energy and the frustrations wrought by a music career that he couldn't fully launch, we might go to the beach in Santa Monica for a swim or head to dinner in Chinatown. He'd always insist on ordering extra dishes so he could have leftovers the next day when he would likely be home in gray sweatpants working on yet another song that might or might not sell. I would sit across from him, savoring my lo mein while he, with his chopsticks punctuating his quick-fire thoughts, told animated stories of potential music-industry connections. Later I would pay the majority of the check, wondering if he would ever be financially stable, and if it even mattered. I could not easily separate my uncertainty about Stefan from the exhilaration of living with him in our gritty downtown loft, of being so alive in my life that the logistics of our relationship, workable or not, mattered less than the adventure. I was twenty-three years old and still waiting to find that path to Japan. Not much mattered to me except escaping my mother, connecting with my dead father, and slaking a nearly unquenchable thirst for the world.

One Friday night in early March, Stefan asked if I'd ever been to the desert.

"No," I told him. "Can you just go to the desert and hang out?"

He looked at me, bemused at first. Then he threw back his head and laughed. "Are you serious?"

That night we drove to the Mojave, following a desolate road into an expanse of sand and sagebrush. We lay on a blanket staring up at the stars and drinking Kahlúa and milk from a cracked silver thermos. "*I want to sleep with you in the desert tonight,*" I sang in an off-key approximation of an old Eagles' line.

"Well you're in luck," Stefan said, and pulled me on top of him, kissing me under that endlessly open sky.

One night after work, I came home to a note on our futon: FOR YOU. PLAY ME. Underneath the handwritten sheet was the portable tape recorder that Stefan used to capture any inspired ideas while on the go. I sat on the edge of the futon and listened to the song he had written called "Hazel Eyes." *Hey hey hey hazel eyes, wanna come and dance in the moonlight?* Afterwards, I clicked off the little battery-run recorder and played the song again up on the roof while gazing at the gush of lights and sorting through my jumbled feelings. Stefan was volatile and broke, impulsive and, at times, impossible to reach through his urgency and tumult of worry. But then he could write a song like this, as if staring right inside me.

When he slipped into bed late that night, I turned so he could see my eyes. "No one has ever written me a song," I whispered.

"It needs work, but for a first try, I think it's pretty good—"

"I love it," I told him. I paused. "And I love you." Just like that, I poured the words into the dark space, the way you might suddenly feel lucky at the roulette wheel and put all of your chips on one number.

"Well I . . ." Stefan began and then, after a moment, said, "have strong feelings for you that I think might be love."

"What might those feelings be, if they aren't love?" I asked, pretending I could roll with it. "Gas?"

"Hmm. Could be gas."

"So, you have strong feelings for me that might be love or might be gas? Is that right?"

"Yep." He smiled at me with his lips zipped, like that was all he had to offer.

It wasn't enough, yet I pretended that it was. Stefan and I had talked about his fear of commitment, spurred perhaps by growing up without ever knowing his biological father, an audiophile of whom he had only one tiny photo, stored in his own box of treasures under his futon. When he showed it to me, something about him made sense in a new way. Wasn't he perhaps searching for his lost father, too?

My own LA trove was growing with twinkly trinkets that offered me nothing conclusive about how to proceed with my life. Outside of my office on Melrose Avenue, I once picked up a glittery Marilyn Monroe magnet. As I studied it, I thought how opposites attract, and how the searcher in me felt drawn to the Hollywood lights. Los Angeles magnetized me, and Stefan was so intimately part of that. But the longer I stayed there, the farther I felt from where I was supposed to be.

Still, I loved my work, and each day was wildly eventful, but none more so, perhaps, than when I sold my first book as an agent: *Red Mist* by an Irish writer named Michael O'Toole. Sherry and I celebrated that night at her favorite sushi bar. It was only the second time I had tried raw fish and didn't much care for the tang of wasabi or the rubbery give of the tuna against my teeth. But for the first time in many months, I revisited my dream to move to Tokyo.

"You know," I told Sherry, who was gobbling her yellow tail like it might swim off the dish. "I've always wanted to go to Japan."

"Me, too, honey," she said. "We should go together sometime. We could visit publishing houses and make it a write-off. Let's do that. Let's go to Japan."

She lifted her porcelain sake cup the size of a large thimble and waited for me to do the same. "To us," Sherry toasted. "You and me, sweetie, and growing this company together." She tapped the rim of her cup against mine. "And to Japan!"

I threw back the rice wine, dissolving my guilt, and then drank another eight cups or so. I'd forgotten how badly I'd wanted Japan just six months earlier when I moved to California, but that night I felt the return of desire, the way I sometimes pressed my palm over my heart, just to feel the engine of my body revving inside my chest.

I got off the bus late that night and searched briefly for Tai Tai. When I didn't see her, I started walking, staggering really, until she strode up beside me. "Can't wait for me? You in a rush, sunshine?"

"Hey there. Sorry," I said, turning fast. Even in the darkness, I immediately noticed her clothes—a man's sport jacket over a T-shirt—unusual for Tai Tai who tended to dress in short shorts with a flashy tube top, the uniform of the LA streetwalker.

She looked down at her chest and then up at me again. "What are you staring at?"

"Your T-shirt," I said, trying not to topple into her. "Is that . . . ?"

She pulled open her jacket, and there across her front was a faded red sun against a stained white background. "You like it?" she said.

"I do," I told her. "It's the rising sun."

She pointed at her chest. "This? This is the rising sun?"

"That's the flag of Japan," I said, my words a fast slur.

"Yeah?"

"I'm *going* to Japan," I told her.

"You serious? That's crazy!" she shrieked. "When you goin' there?"

"Soon, I hope."

"Yeah? Well, I'm gonna miss you."

The following week a letter arrived from my college advisor with a job offer in Japan. I'd be teaching at Obirin University under a two-year contract that included housing, insurance, and a hefty salary paid in yen. I had to give my answer immediately.

When Stefan strode in from his guitar lesson that night, I thrust the letter at him. "I got a job in Japan."

His face twisted. "What?" He read each line slowly, mouthing the words. When he finished he looked up at me, disbelieving. "You're leaving?"

"I've wanted this since I was little. Remember I told you about my father being there?"

His face dimmed as he shook his head. "I don't know what to say. I . . . I didn't know it was so real. You talked about Japan," he continued, "but I didn't know you were actively looking for a job."

"I wasn't," I said. "I kind set this in motion and then let the whole thing go when I came here."

"Are you going to take it?"

"I have to," I said, thinking that's how searches work. When called to adventure, you answer.

On our final night together, sitting on the beach in Santa Monica, Stefan picked up his guitar and played a song he'd written called "Days Go By." There is a line in it that would chafe at my heart for years: *Needing someone who knows why you stay.*

No one ever really knew why I left or stayed because much of my search remained a secret. I wanted love so badly, more than anything really, and that was the bare truth—the truth of all our lives, perhaps. What do we do that isn't for love? Even hatred is the flip side of an open heart. Still I remember the heaviness I felt saying goodbye to Stefan, the first man since my father's death who I had been allowed to love.

23 - SIGHT

On one of my Saturday visits to Connecticut, I found my mother lying in her twenty-five-year-old king-size bed as comfy as a slab of granite, and I stretched out next to her on what had been my father's side.

"What's up, Ma?" I asked. My upbeat tone sounded rehearsed because it was. As she rolled over, I could see purple bruises on her legs and the slack flesh of her calf. Pressed flat on one side, her usually well-coiffed platinum blonde hair looked ready to leap off her head.

"How are you feeling?"

"I'm not good, Sandy. Not good. I was just napping."

I swallowed and tried to rest my fingers on her shoulder. Like putting my hand near a fire, the heat made me pull away fast. We had never deliberately touched or hugged comfortably, and I didn't know how to start. I didn't know how to reach through the dark space between us that had grown ever more forbidding over the decades. The treasure chest in New York City felt far easier to find than a connection with my mother.

I thought of words I had practiced in the car—*Are you afraid to die? Should we talk about what you want . . . in the end?* Instead of actually speaking them aloud, I held them in my mouth and swirled them around. I was pretty sure that a meaningful conversation with my mother, like blow-drying your hair in the bathtub, might cause a fatal shock to my system. Finally I said, "Can I do anything for you?"

She sighed deeply. "Yes, Sandy, you can."

Was she kidding? I could never do anything for her. I mean I could change the high kitchen light bulb while she shouted at me not to fall off the step stool and crack my head open, or I could swap out the autumn wreath for the evergreen one with gold balls and a pink bow. But that was it. She had friends and neighbors who assisted with errands and maintenance companies for repairs. My role began at Rite Aid and ended with lunch at Pizza World that she always paid for.

"What do you need, Ma?"

"I need you to help me drive."

"What?"

"You heard me, Sandy. I want to drive around the block. One last time."

"But you're blind."

She waved me off. "I'm not blind, Sandy!"

"Okay. You're not blind blind, but you're legally blind, which actually sounds worse."

"You think I don't know that?" She put her hand to her head and licked her lips. "I can't even run to the Wawa anymore. What am I supposed to do when I need milk? Cripes!" She turned into the pillow and stayed so still that I feared for a moment that she had died, just expired there in front of me after speaking her last word: *Cripes.* I leaned over, careful not to touch her possibly dead body and studied her mouth for signs of breathing, as I once did with my sleeping babies.

When she pulled her shoulders in tighter, I fell back with unexpected relief that she was, in fact, still alive. "Fine, Ma. Once around the block," I conceded. "But if you go above ten miles per hour, I'm going to kill you."

She trained her rheumy blue eyes on me and grinned menacingly. "Not if I kill you first."

Ten minutes later with the giddy trepidation of a teenager on her maiden voyage behind the wheel, my nearly blind eighty-two-year-old mother settled herself in the seat of her fourteen-year-old impeccably kept white Honda Civic. It had about ten thousand back-and-forth-to-Wawa-for-milk-and-cigarette miles on it.

"Once around the block, Ma," I said. "That's it."

"That's all I need, Sandy."

"Don't go Al Pacino on me."

She snorted. "What was that he kept saying in that movie? Woo woo or something crazy like that?"

"Hoohah!"

"That's it. Hoohah!" She put the car in reverse. "Hoohah!"

"Concentrate, Ma!"

"You act like I don't know how to drive a car."

As she backed out of the driveway at a disturbing angle, veering the rear toward the giant maple that had sequestered my crow on that long-ago day, I grabbed the wheel and pushed it back.

"Who's driving here?" she snapped.

"The blind lady," I said.

I helped her straighten out, but eventually it was mostly my mother, with blurry remnants of vision, who managed to back out onto Lyle Road. How many times had she done this? Pulled out of this very driveway and shot to the store or to the mall for a quick poke through the sale racks? How many times had she left to escape? I figured twice a day for forty-eight years, minus a few vacation and sick days. That would make about thirty thousand backing-outs.

"Now go easy," I told her as I helped her find D on the gearshift.

"I'm going easy, Sandy." She drew a breath and tapped the gas pedal.

For the first few houses on our small block—the Bartelewski's, Ferrara's, and Gervais's—she kept it under ten miles per hour. But somewhere near the Gwozda's, after successfully negotiating two corners and a Buick driven by a wrinkled old bald guy who made my mother look like a college coed, she brought her speed up to fifteen. My hand hovered near the wheel.

As we rounded the last corner that would bring us back to our house, she revved it up even more.

"Do you see that tree, Ma?" I asked.

"Yes, Sandy, I see that tree."

"But you're not driving like you see it!"

"Well, I see it."

"Please brake, Ma! Please brake! Brake!"

Before I could wangle my foot across to the driver's side, my mother stopped hard about four feet in front of the oak. I sat back. "Are you telling me you saw that tree?" I asked.

"Of course I saw it."

"Please just drive home. Slowly!"

"Don't tell me what to do," she said, but then cautiously tapped on the gas pedal and took about three minutes before sputtering into our driveway 100 feet away.

Afterwards, she sat in the car for a long moment, still gripping the wheel and looking ahead at the white garage door. Losing her car meant losing her primary escape hatch out of her own skin and discomfort. She could never open up about her feelings, but she sure could drive away from them.

"Tough to give it up, huh?" I asked.

She nodded and unclipped her seat belt. "Thank you, Sandy."

"Hoohah!" I said.

She tried to smile. "Hoohah!"

24 - SURE

On nights when I got the house to myself, the possibilities plucked at me. After so many years of being mother-on-call at all times, I had just begun to notice the loose ends of my days and how they frayed with uncertainty when Phinny and Addie, both nearly adolescents with growing outside interests, weren't around. It left me with a sense of being both aimless and trapped, and it made me miss them.

One Friday night when Mark was working late, I was flitting from room to room, struggling to find an absorbing project, when David called.

"Argh!" he said. "ARGH!"

"Tell me! What is it? What?"

"Okay. Listen to this." He explained how his cousin Abby in Brooklyn had been doing some reconnaissance for him in a hidden area behind the Brooklyn Public Library in Park Slope. "You have to go behind a fence to the back of the park and then wind along a dirt pathway," he said. "It's weirdly hidden. And, are you ready for this? The exact spot is a few hundred feet from Mount Prospect, the highest site around. You were the one who figured that out."

"That means Mount Prospect would be the ship?" I squealed.

"Exactly. There's even a flagpole on it."

According to David, Cousin Abby had found two distinct, hollowed-out tree stumps, one with a steel shovel and a rake inside, as if begging a treasure hunter to dig there. "You know," David said, "they may as well have put an X on it."

By 6:30 the next morning, we were speeding down the Mass Pike with our travel mugs of French Roast. Mark was still in bed. The kids were at sleepovers. I was finally going guilt-free. Almost.

"How sure are you?" I asked David over "Empire State of Mind," our lucky Brooklyn song that we played to launch our trips. "Ninety-eight? Ninety-nine percent?"

"One-hundred percent," he said. "I'm finally one-hundred percent sure. This place makes perfect sense."

Over the next four and a half hours, we belted out David Bowie songs; we ate vegan crackers that tasted like cardboard with seeds glued on top; and we discussed the vacation David and his girlfriend would take, maybe even to Peru, now that we were really going to find the treasure. When we stopped talking and singing, I quietly prepped for the interviews we'd be giving on New York television stations that night. Had I thought it through better, I would have brushed on a little mascara before leaving the house.

By late morning we were loading our digging supplies into the wheelbarrow and rolling it through the parking lot of the Brooklyn Museum. Around the corner near the entrance to the Botanic Garden, we met up with Cousin Abby, a no-nonsense architectural student in her late twenties and a seemingly excellent addition to our search team. We waited a few moments for a Botanic Garden maintenance woman talking on her phone to someone named Bubby to finish her cigarette and leave. But when she kept going, "Listen to me, Bubby. Bubby! You're not listening!" we nonchalantly sauntered past with our wheelbarrow as if taking a Sunday stroll in Prospect Park with our metal detector and an empty kitty-litter bucket. Ho hum!

After following the length of the paved track, Abby led us to an obscure dirt footpath strewn with cans, bottles, and broken glass. We had to maneuver around a fallen branch to push deeper into the enclave. That's when we saw it: the upright, hollowed-out log, and another right next to it containing the shovel and rake. Rows of pebbles had been artistically arranged on the smoothed-out ground, and the entire place had the peculiar air of an outdoor Wiccan wedding venue. The only sign of civilization was the back view into the offices of the Brooklyn Public Library, closed on a Sunday afternoon.

If the North Forty in Floyd Bennett Field felt strange, we had entered another dimension of New York City weird. What was this place? Did the pirate puppeteers set this all up hoping nobody but us determined treasure hunters would happen upon it?

In spite of David's one-hundred percent certainty, my gut told me they had not. In fact, my gut was saying, *What the hell?*

A light rain began to fall, and, rather unexpectedly, the weather turned bone-chillingly cold. I tucked into myself, feeling idiotic, first for wearing such a thin windbreaker, and then for something else that I saw: a pile of filthy clothes shoved against the chain-link fence. Across the top of the heap, a pair of rain-soaked khakis sprouted feathery blue mold.

"What do you think?" Abby chirped. She was stocky with short brown hair that she shook out of her eyes. She had walked five minutes from her Park Slope apartment. David and I had driven for almost five hours.

"I'm not sure about those clothes," I said, in a moment of gross understatement. The pile was so high it could have been concealing a dead body. I only knew what wasn't under it: a chest full of gold. To David, my voice cutting, I said, "What do *you* think?"

I wanted him to tell Abby that this was so wrong. The whole vibe was wrong. Our would-be benefactors would not have chosen *here* to bury that gold. Couldn't Abby have mentioned the clothes pile yesterday? It was obvious how *not* one-hundred percent right this place was.

"I think" David began, ever the open-minded scientist, "we won't really know until we dig."

"Well, I think it looks like some kind of homeless hideout," I said in a cheerfully nasty tone. "Why else would these clothes be here?"

I fished out the khakis with a stick and dangled them around for everyone's viewing pleasure. When David ignored me and turned toward the hollowed-out log, I let the khakis fall back in the heap.

"Help me," he said and started shoving the log over.

I shook my head at what I knew was a waste of time but played along, truly wanting to be proven wrong.

Once we managed to tip the log, David began poking the shovel into the dirt. Immediately the metal edge met with deeply entrenched roots. No way had anything ever been interred there. In fact, I would have been less surprised to find velociraptor bones than a treasure chest.

"This doesn't make sense," I said while slowly circling the rest of the encampment. On one edge, dead vines thickly matted into shrubbery cascaded over the fence. On the other side, staked seed packets indicated that someone had planted pansies and petunias. I had no idea how they would grow in there without sunlight. In fact, I had no idea about anything anymore, including what I was really looking for.

While David slept, I drove for the first few hours back, regularly slapping my leg and pinching myself awake. Compared to my Saab wagon, driving David's Honda Pilot was like steering a small state.

This was my fourth trip back to Boston empty-handed, and it was time to admit our obsession had become an addiction. I imagined joining a twelve-step program. "Hi! I'm Sandy, and I'm a treasure-hunting addict."

Would anybody understand? How could they? This wasn't about drug abuse or sex addiction or needing to eat an entire box of Double Stuf Oreos, and then putting your fingers down your throat to purge the self-hatred that came with that fullness. It wasn't about alcoholism or obsessive-compulsive disorder or the kinds of things many of Mark's patients dealt with every day. Or maybe it was. Maybe it had to do with growing up lonely in a middle-class, Catholic family, being a fiery young girl forced to endure a home life as empty as that hollowed-out tree stump, with no promise of treasure underneath. And maybe that girl grew into a passionate woman who still obsessively believed her only chance for happiness was buried in some unknowable place.

25 - JAPAN

At twenty-three years old, I stepped off my Japan Airlines flight at Narita Airport in Tokyo and began my life on the opposite side of the world from everyone I knew. Amidst the sea of black-haired strangers, I spotted my name, "Sandy Miller," jotted on a white paper sign, as if someone else had started writing my story in this country.

The young woman holding that sign was Emiko, the secretary from Obirin University's English Department. She appeared so diminutive in her baggy gray pants and white blouse that I instantly questioned how such a slight person could be in charge of me and all my baggage.

Emiko bowed, and, when I offered my hand, she weakly shook my fingertips. Only then did I recall that shaking hands was culturally wrong, but at that point, I felt too foolish to pull back and start bowing. With that one clumsy gesture, I took the first of a thousand missteps in a country that would unfold before me like a cryptic map of a mysterious land.

Fortunately, that day, Emiko, petite though she was, competently led me through the airport to a train, then to another train, and finally to a taxi. Despite my exhaustion, I chatted away, American-style, trying to fill the vacuum of our silence with small talk.

"How many teachers are from the States?"

"Um, maybe just three."

"Do you like working at Obirin?"

She scrunched up her mouth. "Maybe. Yes."

"When will I start teaching?"

"Hmm. Maybe next week."

The day—actually the middle of the night on my body clock—felt like something to survive. As I zoomed ever more deeply into unknown territory, I felt myself missing Stefan, not unlike the way I only really started missing my father after he was gone.

After two hours of traveling and many awkward pockets of strained conversation, Emiko delivered me to a spacious house situated in what seemed to be Tokyo suburbia, streets of tidy, Western-style homes with compact Japanese cars in the driveways.

"I think you will stay here until your apartment is ready," Emiko said. "The school owns this house for visiting professor and, so."

She kicked off her clunky black shoes in the foyer. Following her lead, I did the same before dragging my enormous red Samsonite suitcase inside. She toured me around, "This is kitchen. This is dining room. Bedrooms and restroom are upstairs." She slid her eyes away from mine. We obviously weren't close enough to explore such private territory together. "So," she continued, "maybe I will leave now." With a few more instructions about how to reach her if I needed anything, she was gone. And I was alone.

I circled through the house again, unable to accept that I was there and not at all sure what to do next. I was on my second day of being awake and felt so hungry that I almost wasn't hungry. The cabinet contained tea, a sack of white rice, sugar, soy sauce, and a brown liquid that resembled soy sauce, but, when I poured some onto my finger and tasted, it had a cloying sweetness. I had never in my life made tea with loose leaves and didn't really like the grassy taste of tea anyway. Finally, the appliances confused me, and I feared I only had to push one button on that rice cooker, with its complicated control panel, to make it explode. At that point I would have given anything to be home in my mother's kitchen where there was always a box of rotini pasta in the cabinet and some parmesan and butter in the fridge. But in lieu of the starchy, American comfort food I was craving, I ate a heaping spoonful of sugar sprinkled with soy sauce and headed upstairs to use the bathroom. On the back of the toilet, a sign showed two stick figures. One stick guy was standing *on* the toilet seat facing the wall. There was a big X through him. The other stick guy was *squatting* on the toilet seat—also wrong. Feeling pretty sure I could correctly use a Western-style toilet, I sat down and peed. Then I went into one of the bedrooms, mustered the energy to yank a futon mattress from the closet shelf, and wrestled the migrating bed into place on the pale straw floor.

"I'm in Japan," I said out loud, collapsing onto the stuffed cotton mattress with a pink floral pattern that my mother would have been crazy about. I hugged myself and giggled. "I'm here!"

Although my body was buzzing, my mind raced this way and that, both overtired and exhilarated that I had made good on a decade-long commitment to do this. *Can my father see me now?* I wondered. I trotted back downstairs and rifled through my suitcase until I found the photo I'd taken from the attic trunk over a decade earlier. I looked at my young father, approximately my age, sitting in front of a music memorial somewhere here in this island country. Here! I looked out the window where Japan seemed to be waiting for me. I gathered my courage and ventured out into the hilly neighborhood of neutral-colored houses, not sure what I would encounter. I walked slowly, fearful of going too far into the unknown and then not being able to find my way back home. On the crest of a sloped street, I watched the sunlight fading in the sky, dramatic pink and orange hues, that burned with the same intense palette of sunset on the other side of the Pacific. Was Stefan missing me, too? Did our double futon bed feel as lonely to him as the single mattress I'd be sleeping on that night? I couldn't tell. So far away from the familiar, no intuition or instinct read clear.

Even my father, whose presence I'd expected to feel in Japan, was nowhere to be found in that moment. I shut my eyes and lifted my face to the darkening sky, trying to conjure the man I had struggled to connect with even when we lived in the same house. *Where are you?* I whispered, experiencing nothing in the humid summer air but a sense of my own isolation. Was it foolish of me to think I'd find my father here? Had I ever considered that he didn't even want to be in this country, a place where he was at war?

I opened my eyes and started walking again, trying to move away from my thoughts, not sure if I'd made a mistake in coming here or if it was just the jet lag overwhelming me. I continued on, noting turns and landmarks, but still afraid of getting lost in the maze of sameness. When I passed a home with open blinds, I glimpsed a family of two parents and two young boys sitting at a table sipping from red lacquer bowls. As I furtively watched them, I wondered if I could ever have such ordinary happiness with a husband and children? Would we laugh over dinner? Share the minutiae of our lives in a way that my family never did? I passed by slowly, listening to the indecipherable conversation that launched me even farther away from everyone and everything I'd ever known.

A week later I passed a space-age-looking pay phone kiosk at a Tokyo train station. I had moved from the big suburban house into the University-owned apartment building where I would live for the next two years, but I still didn't have my phone set up. With much uncertainty, I managed to place a collect call, punching in the only phone number I would ever need for my mother, the ten-digit code to her adult life lived in just one place.

"Cripes, Sandy," she answered, her voice gravelly. "Do you know what time it is here?"

I looked at the Timex watch she had sent me as a birthday gift in college. It was four-thirty in the afternoon in Tokyo, which meant twelve hours ahead in Connecticut. "Oh no, Ma." I cringed. "I'm so sorry. I just wanted to call you—"

"That's okay, Sandy. I'm not upset, but it's the middle of the night and, cripes, I can't think straight." I could hear her trying to get oriented, probably switching on the lamp on top of her night-stand. I could practically smell the Nivea lotion.

"I just wanted to say I'm here, Ma. That's all."

"So you're okay? Everything's okay?"

I leaned against the side of the kiosk and exhaled. "I'm okay, Ma. I'm really sorry I woke you. I'll call again at a normal time."

"Okay, Sandy. I just can't even think straight. But I'm glad you're okay. How's Japan, okay?"

"It's okay. I'm adjusting."

"Well, that's good, Sandy. Take care now. I love you."

"I love you too, Ma," I said. It's what I always said when we hung up, just not with my heart. But with the entire earth and a day between us, it no longer felt so frightening to speak those words.

26 - FAMILY

"Do I have to go?" my son whined in that bored teenage drawl that made me flash back on my own annoying adolescent tendencies. Deep into thirteen, Phinny had already turned surly about anything requiring hours in the car with his hyper-inquisitive parents always trying to get a bead on his teenage brain.

"You have no idea what something like this would have meant to me as a kid," I told Phinny as he held his *I'm-not-going* ground. "Grandma Betty didn't take me on treasure hunts. We didn't stay in hotels in New York City. This would have been a dream trip."

"Yeah, well, we obviously have different dreams. Plus, I'm not exactly into pirate treasure."

The night before Patriot's Day—a Massachusetts state holiday in April that commemorates the start of the Revolutionary War—Mark, Addie, and I dropped Phinny with some friends and headed to New York City. I was going to show my family what I'd been working on for almost a year.

"How come we're finally worthy of making this trip with you?" Mark asked as we approached Brooklyn close to midnight, with Addie dozing in the back seat.

"Because," I said, "I want to share this treasure hunt with you."

"Is that it?"

That was it. Mostly. The Boston winter had been stressful without any getaways or breaks beyond my regular weekend visits to New Britain. And while David's interest in the hunt had waned, since he hadn't gathered any new leads, I could not let go of what it meant: an adventure outside of the workaday world, the chance to finally dig up something real. If I felt myself disconnecting from Mark, then this was a way to reconnect us, or so I reasoned.

The next morning, I gazed out the window of our Brooklyn hotel at a day of city sunshine. "Do you hear that treasure calling to us?" I asked Addie, who was still lolling in bed, flipping through the hundreds of channels; a novelty denied her by our cableless television at home.

She rolled her eyes. "Will they have those waffles at breakfast? You know, the kind you pour yourself?"

I smiled at my daughter, who had never met a breakfast carb she didn't love. "Why else do you think I booked this place?"

After coffee and DIY waffles, we walked the half-mile from our hotel through the bustling streets to Grand Army Plaza. "See, that's the Bailey Fountain," I said, pointing at the elaborate bronze statue that figured prominently in the clues. "Check out the pitch-fork and cornucopia, and the man and woman up there represent-ing Felicity and Wisdom. Oh, and that's Neptune. And look, the fountain is a beer volcano. Figuratively, I mean. Remember I was telling you how in the video—"

"No," Addie said. She was already trotting ahead, clearly disinterested in the collection of clues that had captured my imagination.

"You don't remember? Because I—"

"Mom. I *don't* remember," she said, not bothering to turn around. "You care about this stuff, not me."

I watched Mark survey the area. I was trying hard with this trip to bridge the gap between us, but my efforts suddenly felt strained. While my crush on David had weakened as we no longer spent hours together scouring remote corners of Brooklyn—out of sight out of mind had typically served me well with men—I didn't find myself returning to Mark in a meaningful reconnection, one that would preclude my almost habitual need to wander. Rather, I experienced a duality similar to the one that plagued me with my father: the desire to be both seen and to disappear from his gaze. Mark loved me almost effortlessly, never giving me a reason to question his devotion or intentions, but he also liked to keep me close to him, while my own instincts led me to look for holes in fences, to slip away unseen into a dark wood where I could search for my heart with the clarity I could only achieve in those rare pockets of solitude. Even at night when Mark fell asleep before me, I would lie in bed, enclosed in the comfort of darkness, and picture myself searching alone for that treasure chest.

"What do you think?" I asked Mark.

"About what?"

"Can't you practically smell the gold?"

He took a long, deep sniff of the air. "You're saying it could be anywhere here?" He surveyed the area, skeptically.

"Well not anywhere, but around here, or maybe in Prospect Park."

"What about that day last month when you were so sure that you'd found the right spot?"

"Oh that," I said, remembering the ultimately dispiriting trip that led us into the odd sanctuary behind the Brooklyn Public Library. "C'mon, I'll show you where we were."

The pile of clothes was still lying there in a moldy heap, but the carved-out tree trunk we'd tipped over had been righted. "Strange, isn't it?" I said.

"It looks kind of junky in here," Addie said.

"Treasure hunting isn't always pretty. Think of the conquistadors who wiped out ancient civilizations looking for gold. That was bloody and brutal. Or all the pirates who died at sea."

"You know what?" she said. "They should have treasure hunts in malls. Then more kids would do them."

"Honest to God, Addie."

"I'm kidding. But this is really junky. Can we please get out of here?"

Mark turned back toward me. "Yeah, what are we waiting for?" he said gamely. "Show us to the treasure."

"I can't just *show* you to the treasure." I threw up my arms. "It's not that easy."

"Okay, so show us *something*."

Feeling some pressure to amp up the fun, I led them into Prospect Park, a 500 plus-acre expanse of green with a zoo, a boathouse, a carousel, and quite possibly a treasure chest buried somewhere in the vastness. Once there, we combed the fallow areas around and above the Endale Arch, one of the park's five stone sun-sheltering rooms that felt like a reasonable place to conceal a clue. While I peered under the wooden benches inside the arch looking for any encouraging sign—maybe a word encoded in the graffiti on the walls—Addie scampered onto the grassy knoll overhead.

"See anything?" I shouted.

"Nope."

"What about you, Mark?" I asked. He was following our daughter up the embankment.

"I guess I'm still not sure what I'm looking for," he called back. "This feels a little random."

"Well, feeling is important," I said. "Pay attention to anything that *feels* like a clue."

"You know I don't work that way," Mark replied matter-of-factly, reminding me of David and his infuriatingly rational approach to treasure. "Can you give me something more concrete?"

"I don't know if I can," I said. "Maybe today it's about enjoying the search."

"That's cool," Mark said. After a moment, he strolled back into the sun shelter. I was sitting on one of the benches realizing I'd made a mistake in bringing them here. "How long do you want to stay?" he asked. He stood in front of me, his hands on his hips.

"Could you act like you care a little?" I said. "Just pretend."

Mark reached out his hand and set it on my shoulder. His eyes met mine. "I'm here with you because I care," he said. "And I'm also thinking about rush hour traffic."

I huffed. "So why don't we just leave now."

"Why are you suddenly turning this into an argument?"

"I'm not."

"Yes, you are. We've been having a perfectly nice day here. It's fun to see what's got you so obsessed."

"Is that what you think?" I stared into his eyes, which, in that moment, hardly felt familiar. "I'm obsessed?"

"A little bit. Yeah. Is that wrong?"

I walked out of the arch and into the glaring afternoon sunshine. "No," I said. He was right, but I hated that he put it that way. *Obsessed* to a psychologist was a diagnosis, half of a mental illness. "Let's just drive home. This is obviously not something that interests you."

He turned me toward him. "Okay, since you asked, that's right. I can't say I see anything here that indicates it would lead us to treasure. But you seem pretty set on making this place work. Honestly, I think you're on a wild goose chase, but I'm also happy to indulge you."

"Let's just go," I said.

"We don't have to go."

"Yes, actually we do."

He held my arm. "Why?"

"Because I think I have to figure this out alone."

"Figure what out?"

I squeezed my eyes shut against the tears. "Whatever the hell it is I'm doing here."

I walked away from him, remembering all the times I'd been obsessed with searching, how in Japan I began to carry the photo of my father everywhere, hoping to find the music monument, looking for the connection to some place my dad had stood forty-three years earlier. I showed the picture to all of the English-speaking professors at my school. "Do you know where this could be?" I asked. "That's my father in World War II."

My Japanese boss, the head of the English Department, stared at the photo, sucking air in a show of uncertainty. "So, so, so. Maybe this is Tokyo, but maybe this music memorial is not there any longer."

There were so many memorials that had been destroyed, but my beginner-level Japanese language skills limited my ability to search at libraries or ask probing questions at historical sites. I simply couldn't make myself understood. Without the diary, I didn't even know where my father had been stationed, and at times, I seemed to be hunting for a ghost of a soldier that only existed inside of me. Still carrying that photo around made me believe that, true to my intention for moving to Japan, the people we've lost could return to us in the most unexpected ways. We just had to stay alert to what the world offered. That photo of my father led me to places that imprinted on my soul, like the evergreen forest surrounding the Meiji Shrine in Tokyo. I would wander amongst the trees that smelled like Christmas and loss, remembering our yard growing up and my father's beloved blue spruce that stood like a sentinel outside my bedroom window. I also climbed Mount Takao one day just to visit the Yakuoin Temple, home of the Japanese crow gods. As I gazed out at the impossibly lush mountain scenery with *Tengu*, a lucky crow-like figure watching over me, I felt the strange blessings of my search. I thought of the crow that flew off with my heart when I was young. I thought of how our truest searches, if we decide to undertake them, lead us to the most astonishing places. And every day that I lived in Japan, no matter what I found—or didn't—I felt a small, sharp sense of gratitude for my father, who had led me there.

27 - SEA GLASS

A few weeks after the family trip to New York City, I was driving to New Britain to take my mother to the doctor when, realizing there were hours to spare before the afternoon appointment, I made a significant detour to Hammonasset Beach. The largest state park in Connecticut contained the farmland where my father grew up in a rambling house with his six siblings and a barnful of animals. After he died, the campground there was named in honor of his environmental legacy, most notably, erecting a stalwart row of sand dunes to protect the beach from watery doom. Living in Japan at the time, I couldn't attend the dedication ceremony, but I went to the park one day each year and stood before the sign that read: WILLIAM F. MILLER CAMPGROUND. I didn't move on, not until I felt a softening in my heart for my father, who didn't know how to raise daughters but understood well how to fight for things that mattered to the environment.

That day I walked a mile down the stretch of beach on Long Island Sound, barely able to lift my eyes from the sand for fear of missing something: a colorful rock, a translucent gold shell, a bit of glass, a broken beach toy, a coin polished smooth by the sea. In his top dresser drawer, my father had a cardboard jewelry box filled with more than a dozen rings that he had found when surveying the shoreline for damage after storms. When my mother was out of the house, I loved to stir those rings around, or try them on, sometimes all at once so my fingers clinked out a dull metallic tune. When my father died, the box disappeared, like everything else.

On our family beach vacations with Mark and the kids at a cottage in Rhode Island, I walked for miles, often stopping to squat in the rocky trim along the water's edge and sift my hand though the pebbles in search of sea glass.

"I never find any," Mark said one day, squatting beside me, trying to spy one jewel-colored shard among thousands of tiny, slick stones.

"If you think you won't find it, then you won't," I told him, emphatically. "You have to believe treasure is out there."

"Whatever it is," Mark said, "I just don't ever find it." He kissed my cheek and trotted back down the beach.

All these years later, as I prowled the Connecticut shoreline for treasure, I had to remind myself to appreciate the experience of the search and not just focus on a desired outcome. *Don't let yourself feel devastated when the tide takes your bit of blue glass before you can reach down and catch it. Don't stand there regretting what you missed. At least you can say that you tried.*

I certainly tried with sea glass and that treasure chest in Brooklyn, but was I trying with my mother? *What if she dies soon?* I asked myself. *Could I have tried harder?*

When I brought a luminous green piece of sea glass to her that afternoon, she jokingly pinched the emerald-colored fragment between her fingers and pretended to pop it in her mouth.

"Is it good?" I asked.

"Yeah, good," she said. "Greens are healthy." She cackled. "It tastes a little crunchy, though."

"Do you like it? Really? I found it for you."

"Sure. It's nice, Sandy. Now what should I do with it?"

"Put it on the windowsill," I said, "and think of me when you look at it."

She laughed and said, "I'll do that."

Later that evening I drove away knowing that she thought of me often with care packages and cards, usually with some cash inside and a note that read, "Buy something you need." When Mark and I were faced with a daunting expense, she might send a more significant check that I would deposit in our bank account with appreciation, as well as a small pinch of resentment. I was always grateful for her generosity and told her so, but it also felt like hush money, as if she was buying my silence around what she couldn't give emotionally.

And what exactly did I need? For her to accept the broken gifts I offered? For her to tell me that I was enough and could stop looking for treasure to prove my worthiness? Yes and yes, I thought as I watched the clouds change shape above the highway. A tree. A dragon. A shell. An X. Always an X.

At home that evening, I went straight to my computer to check on the hunt as I did every day. It was more than one and a half years after the first YouTube video had been posted, and David and I had been hoping that at some point the pirates would try to reignite interest by releasing another clue. The treasure hadn't been found and no one, according to the online message boards, seemed to be making fresh progress. Although the Facebook page occasionally received a comment or a small flurry of activity, the hunt appeared to be stagnating in a way that felt almost heartbreaking to me. What if the treasure was never found? Without telling David, I wrote a pleading e-mail to the "pirate puppeteers" at the contact address on their website. I begged them to release one more clue, asking: *Take pity on this desperate old scallywag, would you, mateys?*

I never heard back.

28 - ALCHEMY

For Mother's Day a few weeks later, I cruised my mother around New Britain, her hometown for eighty-three years. We drove to my grandparents' still-beige house a mile from ours on Anise Street and pulled up to the curb in front. My grandmother had been a stabilizing fixture in my childhood, but not enough to right the imbalance created by my parents' capricious moods and behavior.

"I miss Granny," I told my mother.

"Me, too," she said.

"What about Poppy?" I asked. I thought of my grandfather who had died of stomach cancer when I was nine. He had work-roughened hands with thick, grease-stained knuckles. I remember the strength of his grip on my rib cage when he would reach for me and lift me onto his lap.

"What *about* Poppy?" she snapped.

"Were you close to him?" I asked.

"Oh yes. We would get up early together in the morning, and I'd help him in his workshop. Just the two of us."

"What did you do?" When I turned to look at her, she stared through the windshield at the now weathered home where she had grown up with two adoring brothers, one older, one younger.

"Well, I don't remember exactly, Sandy."

"Did you talk? Or have breakfast first?"

"I don't know. Sometimes I helped him with his business." She waved me off. "Stop asking so many questions."

"Tell me about the clips."

"Now, Sandy, I've already told you a hundred times."

"Tell me again. Please."

"Well, he had that patent for these metal clips that went onto the snow chains that wrapped around tires, then locked them in place. I would help him address the envelopes and put the metal clips inside. We got orders from all over the country."

"So small metal things are in my blood," I said.

"What's that supposed to mean?"

"I like finding things," I said. "Pieces of metal. Coins. Stuff like that."

"You always did. Cripes those things you used to collect. I still have all that stuff jammed in boxes in the back of your closet."

"Ma?"

"What, Sandy?"

"Actually, never mind."

"What do you mean, never mind?"

I hesitated. I didn't know how to say it, how to ask her about a memory of my grandfather that had recently punctured my consciousness. Looking at the house, I could see the window of the bedroom where I was sleeping the night of the Donna Lee Bakery murders. Down the hall, under the slanted eaves, was a narrow storage space where my grandfather's hunting rifles hung on pegs. Beneath the rifles on a bear pelt rug was a stack of *Playboys* that I'd sometimes rifle through, both fascinated and ashamed as I tried to understand the hushed secrecy of female bodies. Two floors down, in his basement workshop, my grandfather had a picture of an old-fashioned, bosomy pin-up girl, her red bathing suit a singular bright spot on the otherwise dark walls.

"Sometimes I thought Poppy was a little . . . unusual," I said hesitantly. I wanted to say *creepy*, but I knew she would shut me down.

"Honest to God, Sandy, I don't know where you come up with these things!"

"Was he nice to you?"

My mother nodded her head, still gazing at her childhood home, a place that likely held her own carefully locked trove of secrets. "He used to get up with me every morning . . . ." Her voice trailed off. "Of course he was nice to me. He was my *father*."

I looked back at the house not telling her what I remembered.

———

"What are these?" my grandfather asked, poking at my still flat, little-girl nipples, not yet blossoms on my chest. I drew away from his finger, but he held me tighter against his coarse flannel work shirt.

"You don't know what these are?" he asked, pointing again at my chest, this time touching me through my pink T-shirt. He wore thick glasses that magnified his eyes and had tan plastic hearing aids with a wire connecting them. He looked broken.

"I don't know," I said. I felt my face redden. He laughed. Up close I could see the gray stubble on his chin and smell his sour breath. In that moment, I hated my grandfather.

"You don't know?" he said. "You don't know what these are?"

I shook my head. He was still pointing, even as I tried to hunch my shoulders forward and pull my chest back from his finger.

"These are your goose bumps."

"Oh," I said, because I couldn't be impolite to any adult, certainly not my grandfather.

When he laughed again, his arms loosened enough that I could wriggle away. I bolted upstairs to my mother's childhood bedroom where, once I caught my breath, I lost myself in stacks of white boxes and drawers full of things I had found before. I closed my eyes on the beauty of handkerchief boxes and sniffed the insides of my grandmother's vinyl pocketbooks that she would forever be "saving for best." I shook out coins and clasped them in my fist to keep from crying.

I did not go into Grandfather's storage room next door with the brown rifles pegged to the wall and magazines with naked women on the floor. I did not even think about it that day.

Without knowing, I imagined how it might have been for my mother. *Is that what happened?* I wanted to ask. *Tell me something, anything, so I can forgive your absence and stop this endless search.*

29 - DOWN

On a ride to Rite Aid the following Sunday, my mother kept swiping her frail, age-spotted hand over the dashboard. "Cripes, Sandy. This car is so filthy, I don't know how you even drive it."

"Just because a car is filthy, that doesn't make it hard to drive," I informed her.

"I wouldn't be so sure."

In Rite Aid, she used a coupon to buy two Snickers bars for her hairdresser, Frankie. She also had a coupon for an eight-ounce bag of almonds, but they'd run out, so she took a rain check entitling her to buy the product for the discounted price once they had restocked. I had never seen anyone younger than seventy-five exercise this option.

"What a nuisance," my mother said. "Audrey loves those almonds. I wanted to give them to her after church tomorrow."

"I'll bring you back next Saturday," I promised.

"We'll see," she snipped, like it was some kind of privilege for me to drive two hours from Boston and spend the afternoon in one of the crappiest drugstores on the East Coast.

Back in my mother's neighborhood, she clutched my arm as I walked her around the block. She would shuffle along next to me and then suddenly high step over a bump on the sidewalk. "I'm afraid I'll go flying, Sandy." She toed the ground with her off-white orthopedic shoes.

We continued on, ploddingly, my mother, completely reliant

on me, a different person from the woman who used to zip around these same sidewalks, paces ahead, terrified that I'd catch her with my needs and questions. Except for her indomitable sass, this fragile old woman was almost unrecognizable as I guided her along, trying to be gentle with her broken parts. How was it that I felt immune to this decline, even as middle age staked its claim on my own body in the form of gray hairs, looser skin, age spots on my hands, a general slowing down, and flabbiness?

I studied the soft folds along my mother's jawline and her hair, ever a golden confection atop her head. We were both Scorpios, both born of the Dragon in Chinese astrology, thirty-six years apart. I always wanted for us to have nothing in common and struggled to admit that we did. Walking together, I couldn't help but recognize what we shared: steeliness as we aged, the need to keep putting one foot in front of the other, no matter how awful we felt. Even her worry for my dirty dashboard felt strangely similar to my concern for my own children's messy rooms.

Back at her house in the fading afternoon light, we sat at the kitchen table and drank Sanka from stoneware mugs. As my gaze followed that hand, frail and spotted, unsteadied by age, I saw what I used to see: the way she would raise it to slap me or wave a cigarette through the air as she accused me of being an ungrateful brat. It took a lot for me to remember that those same hands also picked flowers from my father's gardens and cooked thousands of beautiful meals, and every evening before bed, my mother clasped those hands together in prayer, but for what? What was my mother praying for? I tried to extend my own hand across the table and reach for her, but I couldn't; instead I got unbearably tired. Not *real* tired, but that other kind when you need to shut your eyes on something that you can no longer stand looking at.

"I need a nap before I drive home," I told my mother.

"Good idea," she said. "You don't want to fall asleep at the wheel."

Upstairs in my shrimp-colored bedroom, I peeled back the polyester bedspread that adhered like a scab to the pink blanket beneath it and collapsed on the Navajo-themed sheets. My room still held remnants of my travels, a painting of a cherry branch I'd sent my mother from Japan and a watercolor of Luxembourg, where I lived for the next several years. I thought of all the time I spent on the other side of the world, as far from this place as I could get.

I turned away from the memories nailed to the walls of my bedroom and rolled out of bed. I pried open one of the windows as far as it would go and climbed out onto the first-floor roof. From the edge, I inspected the distance to the ground: about nine feet. I had never jumped but always wanted to, if only for the feeling of a dramatic escape from my staid house where my version of fun was resolutely frowned upon. I flipped around, grabbed the slight overhang of shingles, and let myself fall into the bed of pachysandra that my father had planted some thirty years earlier. I stood up, brushed myself off, and looked around for what to do next. It took me a moment to realize where I needed to go.

I bolted across our lawn and down Hazelmere Road, and then turned into the woods. I forged my way over roots and fallen limbs to The Brook, where Betsy and I had launched our bottle on a long-ago summer day. It was one of those places that had sheltered me in childhood, and here it was, almost unchanged, as if waiting for my return, eager to show me something that I'd forgotten or— through so many years—refused to look at.

The Brook ran low after a dry spell, and I hopped easily onto a few stepping-stones before leaping up onto Treasure Island. I squatted down on that protruding granite boulder and lowered my fingers into the cool water, touching those weeks and months and years of my life given over to searching.

What, if anything, had changed since I came here as a child, fleeing the fire of my mother's and father's rage? Had anything I'd done in my life brought me closer to recovering what I had lost as a child, or did I just need the courage to stop looking?

Later, on my way out of the woods, I spotted a thick, Y-shaped branch from the ground, and picked it up, thinking Phinny might want to turn it into a slingshot. In addition to swearing, he loved to blow things up or strike them with rocks. But as I held up the branch, I remembered something else from so long ago that the memory felt more like a dream—my father pacing our front lawn using a Y-shaped stick like this one to try to find water. I stopped to fully consider what I had seen that day; then I laughed out loud as an idea occurred to me.

30 - FORETELLING

Sitting on the window seat of Mark's study overlooking the budding mulberry trees in our backyard, I huddled under a thick afghan. Winter had fully melted into spring, but the chill of many cold months in our house—weather-wise and emotionally—continued to linger. I had a map of Brooklyn neighborhoods laid out in front of me and was staring at it with focused intention.

Not only did Mark and Addie not catch the gold fever as I had hoped they might on our March afternoon in Brooklyn, but they seemed less interested than ever in the treasure hunt. Inversely proportionate to their lack of enthusiasm, my passion to find the gold had only intensified. As long as the treasure chest was out there, I could enter my day with a sense of possibility. But that meant I had to actually keep searching in some productive way.

I wrapped myself more tightly in the blanket and carefully picked up a silver chain with a pink, tear-shaped pendulum dangling from the end. I'd bought it years ago when a spiritual bookstore in my town was going out of business. Until now, I had no reason to use it.

A week before when the memory of my father pacing our yard with the upside-down slingshot resurfaced, I went online to research dowsing, the nebulous art and science of energetically discovering things. It seemed that my father's dowsing technique of utilizing a forked stick to locate water dated back thousands of years, possibly to Biblical times when Moses and Aaron talked about using a "rod" to find water. I also learned that one could dowse for insight, wisdom, internal energies, oil, minerals, missing people, and—drumroll, please—buried treasure. Beyond the "slingshot" method, there were multiple techniques to try. A person could even hire professionals, like dowsing doctors, with specialties such as silver mines or iron ore. My father, I began to believe, had an instinct for sensing water, although the online literature said that dowsing had less to do with simply finding something than tapping an ancient source of knowledge and earth energy.

Me? I just wanted that treasure, and David's logical approach wasn't getting the job done. So, I decided to experiment, not mentioning in our sparse communication that I was going rogue.

Cobbling together instructions from a dowsing website, I felt drawn to the method that employed a pendulum, mostly because I already owned that pink one. So, no purchase necessary! Following the online suggestions, I used a pencil to divide my map of Brooklyn into squares on a grid, and after the recommended prayer for guidance, began.

Grasping the chain, I held my rose quartz pendulum over Prospect Park and watched as the stone went from stillness into a gentle sway. I continued to work my way around the area, with the pendulum sometimes swinging off-course. Was I moving it or unconsciously influencing the direction? How would I even know? Basically, after just twenty minutes, I felt bored, not to mention rather dubious about the whole thing, but I pushed myself to continue what I'd taken the time and trouble to set up.

As the pendulum moved north to south and back again, I imagined myself calling David, the consummate scientist and saying, *I know where the treasure is. I dowsed it.*

You what?

Dowsed.

Yeah, I don't think so.

When I got no conclusive activity around Grand Army Plaza, I held the stone over Floyd Bennett Field, our very first digging site, the one where David and I got caught by police headlights in the North Forty.

Immediately the quartz reacted, swinging in jagged swirls over the place we had eliminated a year ago. Which meant what? That my hand was shaking? That the North Forty in Floyd Bennett Field was the correct spot? That there is an indiscernible line in the world between wishing and reality, and it's anyone's guess how they interconnect? When I tried to go back and re-dowse places on the map, I only grew more confused and finally gave up after an hour or so.

I e-mailed David later that week, just to ask how he was doing. He wrote back that he was busy with work, kids, life. When I proposed we get together and look at how all the clues aligned from the beginning, he responded, "Sure. After I finish this grant application in a couple of weeks."

A few days later I came across the Brooklyn map again. Without using the pendulum, I shut my eyes and let my hand skim the air above it, dabbling my fingers around. When gut instinct told me to stop, I stilled my hand and looked down in the same intuitive, if random, way that I collected things on the ground. *Maybe that hairbow is telling me to be more childlike. Perhaps that round silver washer is a reminder of my wholeness.* My fingers hovered above Green-Wood Cemetery. Seconds later I was at my desk Googling.

I called David. "I think it's in Green-Wood Cemetery," I said. "We have to go there."

A sigh punctuated his silence. I'm sure my random approach to treasure hunting made him roll his eyes, or worse. But for me, the best answers came in the most surprising ways. Gut instinct had led me around the world, and I wasn't about to stop listening to those inner messages because of my partnership with an inveterate scientist.

"I'm still convinced there's some Morse code thing that we're missing," David mused.

"Well," I said, "Samuel Morse *is* buried in Green-Wood Cemetery."

"Fine. But no one buried the gold there. They aren't going to send people digging around in a cemetery."

"You can't be sure," I said.

"I'm pretty sure."

"You won't come with me to Green-Wood to look?"

"I'm sorry, but no."

"Then I'm going without you," I said. "And I'm going to find it."

31 - RAW

After my day of dowsing, I spent more than forty bucks on a used coffee table book titled *Brooklyn's Green-Wood Cemetery: New York's Buried Treasure*, a title that I, of course, took to be a sign. The jacket flap quoted an 1866 *New York Times* article: "It is the ambition of every New Yorker to live upon Fifth Avenue, to take his airings in the (Central) Park, and to sleep with his fathers in Green-Wood."

When the book arrived and I read it through for clue possibilities, I sensed, without really knowing, that I had "finger dowsed" an intriguing place worth exploring. It made me think that if my father, a man of faith and reason, could successfully employ an unorthodox method to find water, then maybe I, too, had the ability to uncover what I was looking for.

"In the next few weeks I need to spend some time with my mother," I told Mark that evening as we were preparing dinner, a task we each accomplished well enough on our own but struggled with in tandem. "Maybe a night or two."

"That's fine," he said, using a steak knife and a fork to cut raw chicken for soup while I held back from suggesting a more efficient method. "How's Betty doing?"

"Not too well. She's tired all the time and out of breath. I wish she'd think about assisted living, or at least downsizing."

"Maybe I should go with you next time. We can talk to her together." My mother had always adored Mark, often acting like he was the one thing I did right in my life. She would address our

Christmas cards to my husband—making sure to include the "Dr." title before his name—"and Sandy," as if forgetting that I had a different last name, not to mention my own identity. Sometimes Mark felt like the son she wanted more than a second daughter, who pushed her buttons and refused to play nice.

"Not this time, but thanks," I said casually. "She and I have some stuff to sort out."

"How are *you* doing with everything?" His tone was cautious, as he focused on sawing the rubbery chicken thigh into one-inch cubes.

"I'm fine," I answered, stirring the onions that didn't need stirring. "Sort of."

"I know you're going through a lot with her." He didn't look up, just kept cutting. "But I want you to know I miss you."

"I miss you, too."

"I feel like you keep getting farther away, though."

I pretended not to hear over the sizzle of onions. I didn't want to talk about how far away I'd gone or how I was always expected to come back. I took care of the kids with all of the attention I could muster, and I got my writing work done. But I still pulled at the tether of restrictions that exist within a marriage. I wanted to leave without leaving. I wanted to find myself without losing my family, only I couldn't figure out how.

After leaving Japan, I moved to Europe with a man who wasn't my soul mate. And here I was in a marriage with Mark, who I believed was my soul mate, grappling with a different issue: wanting to be held close, as strong as an instinct to wriggle away into my own dark woods, to indulge this longing that burned from inside, as potent and real as those shiny yellow pieces of onion stinging my eyes until they filled with tears.

32 - ACCUSE

"This sandwich is very good, Sandy," my mother said. We were eating lunch across from each other at her shiny black kitchen table.

"I'm glad," I said, as I mindlessly nibbled at my lunch. I was staying at her house that night and heading to Brooklyn the next day.

When I told my mother that I was going to look for the treasure on my own, she said, "Well, good luck with that!"

After lunch, I went into the living room and peered through the sliding glass door out at the dogwood tree. The birdfeeder had been gone for decades, but I could still remember how it lured my crow to me that day.

My mother peeked into the room. "What are you staring at?" she asked.

I swallowed hard. "Will you do me a favor, Ma?" I said.

"Sure? You want me to go find you some treasure?"

"Sort of. Not really."

I walked over to the dining room table and pulled out the chair at the head of the table, the place my father had been sitting all those years ago. "Could you just sit down here for a minute?"

"Sit down? Why?" she asked. "What are you going to do, tie me up?"

When I led her over to the chair, she finally surrendered and tentatively lowered herself into the chair. "Now what, Sandy? Are you going to put on a show?"

"No," I said. "But I need you to be quiet. Just for a minute. Okay?"

"Okay." She started flipping through the pile of junk mail on the table. "I would sure like to know what this is all about."

"Just give me a minute, Ma. One minute?"

"Fine. You can have one minute. And don't think I'm not counting."

I hurried to my place at the window. With my mother loudly shuffling papers, I shut my eyes and journeyed back forty-three years to the moment that crow flew away with my heart. Time collapsed and, once again, I was a five-year-old girl standing in that room, with my mother and father fuming behind me. I felt the beige carpet against my bare toes and the cold wall of glass, enclosing me in my most visceral childhood memory. That day I felt my heart split apart from theirs. That day I began to outgrow my parents' stifling spirits and believe in the power of treasure to save me.

With my mother sighing heavily, I waited for something to happen. I willed a crow to land in front of me in a full reenact-ment of the moment when my search began in earnest. But no bird came. No sign appeared. I just stood there, gazing at the late spring sky, impeccably blue and cloudless. I no longer understood what I was looking for.

My mother huffed. "Sandy. What are you up to? Am I sup-posed to sit here all day?"

I ignored her, desperate to understand what it was that I needed from her. I'd spent my childhood wishing that everything at home could be different, but maybe it didn't work that way. Maybe nothing had to change. Maybe I had the right parents and had lived exactly the right life. Look at all of those places I had visited and all the people I had loved—even the ones who hurt me, *especially the ones who hurt me*. Weren't those the ones who taught me the hardest lessons? Maybe I didn't need anything else, and what we had together was enough. *It has to be,* I told myself *because I don't have a choice.*

My mother looked up from the mail. "Are you going to tell me what you're staring at, Sandy?"

I turned fully around. "I'm looking at you," I said. "Now let's go for a walk."

"A walk? Cripes, Sandy, I can hardly stand up straight. But fine. If that's what you want, we'll go for a walk."

Back at her house after our walk, my mother began pulling clothes from her closet and pressing me to try them on—a long, yellow, polka-dot dress and a black Yves Saint Laurent bathing suit with a gold buckle. They didn't fit right, but I didn't care. I said I wanted them.

"Now don't take these things unless you are going to wear them, Sandy."

"I'll wear them," I promised. Of course I had no intention of ever wearing a backless polka-dot gown or a bathing suit from the sixties, but I gladly accepted them anyway. I took everything she offered me.

"And I want you to clear out those boxes in your closet with all your doodads," she urged. "You even have things in there from Japan, I think."

"Not today, Ma," I said. "I'll get them next time."

33 - GRAVITY

After four harrowing hours of traffic from my mother's house in Connecticut to Brooklyn, I drove through the Green-Wood Cemetery's Gothic revival gates with wild green parrots nesting in the turrets overhead.

"C'mon," I had said to David on the phone the week before. "Wild parrots? On a pirate treasure hunt? How is that not a clue that this could be the right place?"

"I'm not buying it," he said. "But if you find the gold in that graveyard, it's all yours." If only he knew how little I cared about the money.

Once inside the gates, I focused on getting to the Sugar King's gravesite that, according to an online map, was shaped like the footprint clue in the first video. I drove and stopped, getting myself lost in eddies of numbered plots and small pathways that encircled exotic trees and crumbling white marble crosses. I scanned the trees for crows, knowing that mythologically they are messengers from the underworld, cemetery dwellers with plumage as black as death. But none appeared beyond the one that lived vividly in my memory. Finally, I made my way to the Sugar King's mausoleum dug into a hill with a steep crest upon which the rest of his family was buried. Nothing. Not a clue. No code near Samuel Morse either. I looked around in vain before driving to a place called Battle Hill, a name not lost on me as everything around this treasure hunt had begun to feel like a fight. I trudged up a narrow path to the top where a grand statue of Minerva, the Roman goddess of war, wisdom, poetry, and magic waved across Hudson Bay to Lady Liberty. Sitting on a bench above that cemetery, I stared out at the clear blue sky and down at the New York Harbor, thinking how small I felt and how little I knew about anything at all, especially death. Isn't death the one puzzle that the living can never solve, more unknowable than dark matter, than the mysteries of love, than what to say to your distant mother, or to your husband, who can't keep you from drifting away?

Mark and I were struggling, still. Or, rather, I was struggling as he continued to reach for me. He didn't even know I was in New York and thought I was at my mother's house, helping her with spring-cleaning. I didn't tell him because I didn't want his doubt dampening my faith in treasure. *You're going where? To a cemetery in Brooklyn? Alone?*

Everything in marriage required conversation and consensus. Sometimes I imagined a secret escape route that no one could obstruct. I wanted to drive as far as I could in a day, stopping only when I needed a break, and then hitting the gas pedal and journeying on. In deciding to marry and have children, I had waived my ability to leave completely on my own terms. Ever.

When our children were little, Mark and I sometimes had explosive arguments, usually about both of us needing more free time (once in a shamefully low moment, I threw down his eyeglasses and stomped on them), but then, like always, we would fight our way back to each other because we didn't have the luxury of time to do otherwise. With young ones to attend to, there was always another banana that needed peeling, another diaper that needed changing. Now, in middle age, with two kids in middle school gaining independence from us, we could easily let things fester.

The weekend before I had been huffing down the bike path walking off an argument, when a high-strung cyclist, heading in my same direction, circled around and came to a quick halt in front of me. "Is this the beginning or is it the end?" he asked, his words clipped with impatience.

I looked at him for a second and laughed. "Of what? The bike path? Life? Is this an existential question?"

"No," he said with flat annoyance. "Which way is the long way? I want to ride the length of the path, and I need to know where it is."

I pointed in the direction that he had not been heading. "That way," I said. "It's about twelve miles to Bedford."

He brusquely thanked me and pedaled off.

I walked home and broke my standoff with Mark by telling him about the guy's question. "Isn't that a funny way to approach somebody? 'Is this the beginning or the end?' Who says that?"

"Like that seventies song," Mark said. He started singing in an off-key falsetto. "*Are we in love or just friends? Is this my beginning or is this the end?*"

"So, which is it?" I turned to avoid his gaze. "Is this the beginning or the end?"

"Neither," Mark said blithely, not letting my crisis drag him down, too. "It's the middle. And you always say that the middle is the long, hard part of a story."

My mind beamed north from Green-Wood to a different cemetery halfway between New York and Boston: St. Mary's Cemetery, across from the Rite Aid in New Britain where, just yesterday, my mother and I were prowling the aisles with her worn envelope full of coupons. Before driving back home to Boston, I would often take a detour to St. Mary's and stand alone at my father's gray granite headstone, the size of a shirt box. Next to it was an empty plot where my mother would one day be buried. What did they have at the end of thirty-two years together? I knew almost nothing of their marriage beyond the annoyance regularly on display in our home. Did they love each other beneath their ever-simmering anger? Did they even once make love again after conceiving kids? He died when she was fifty-eight, and she never dated again. What if Mark were dead in ten years, when I was fifty-eight? What would life be without him beside me, cracking bad jokes, holding me with such tenderness? I loved Mark. I loved his full mouth and stupid songs and outsized capacity to forgive. He could be stubborn and blameful sometimes, but so could I.

I looked over my shoulder at Minerva, thinking she, the goddess of wisdom, might say something astute about this situation. Instead I heard my mother's words coming from Minerva's white stone mouth: *Cripes, Sandy! What are your looking for anyway?*

I laughed at first, and then started to cry, choking when I thought of my mother and the distance between us that I could never breach, and knowing I had to be okay with that. It had to be enough. But with Mark I had a choice. I reached for my phone.

"Hey," he answered. "What's up? How's Betty?"

"I'm in New York," I said.

"You're what?"

"I stayed at my mom's last night and drove to Brooklyn today. I'm sorry I didn't tell you."

"What are you doing in New York?"

"David said they'd never bury a chest of gold in a graveyard, but I didn't believe him."

"So, wait? Did you find the treasure?"

"No. I wish," I said, looking out at the harbor. "I'm just sitting here alone in this gorgeous old cemetery in Brooklyn." I stopped to take a breath and feel the spring breeze on my face. "And I got scared that I might lose you when—"

"When?"

"When I love you so much."

"I love you so much, too."

"But I had to come here to realize that I'm not mad at you, really, I'm just sad, and confused about my mother."

"So why do you keep disappearing?"

"I'm still looking for something. Not the treasure." I started crying so hard that I knew he couldn't even tell what I was saying. "I've been looking for my mother my whole life, and I should be able to find her . . ."

"Did something happen?"

"No. But . . ." I started crying harder. "Do you know I can count on one hand the times we've had a real connection? But I have to be okay with that, or I'll never be okay."

"Oh, sweetheart, I don't know what to say."

"I don't want her to die, Mark. What if she dies today, and I'm here in New York looking for treasure? Or tomorrow? She's going to die, soon, and then what?"

"You might never have her the way you want her, but you will always—and I mean *always*—have me."

I nodded and whimpered. I was crying so hard I could hardly speak. "Don't ever die," I said to him, remembering how Phinny at age five would make me promise exactly that every night before bed. *Never,* he would say.

"I won't die," Mark said. "Not today anyway. But you need to come home."

"I want to come home," I said. "But I don't want to give up on her, you know? I don't want to stop looking for her."

"You don't have to," Mark said. "But you do have to stop leaving."

34 - RING

On my way back to Boston, I swung by my mother's house for a brief visit and found her lying in bed watching *Jeopardy*. She never missed the show, not even on holidays. If she were on the phone at 7:30 p.m. talking to Alex Trebek himself, she'd ask him to call back in a half hour.

"Come on in, Sandy," she said as I stood in the doorway. "Did you find the treasure?"

"Nope." I plopped down next to her, feeling the weight of my frustration sink into the mattress.

"Well that's too bad." She turned her focus back to the TV. "Now this gal on the right is quite sharp. I think she's going to win it."

"Yeah?" We watched together for another ten minutes. As predicted, the sharp gal made bank.

When the show ended, my mother clicked off the television and sighed into the silence. She didn't move for a long time before rocking herself up to sitting. Once she'd caught her breath, she stood and slowly made her way across the room to her built-in white dresser.

"What are you doing, Ma?"

She yanked open the top drawer and started pawing through the tangles of costume jewelry she had accrued over the decades. "Cripes. I can't see a thing."

"What are you looking for?"

"There's a red box in here somewhere."

I dashed over and placed my hand right on the tiny velvet box—more burgundy than red, with a slightly scuffed lid. I knew it well.

"How did you find that so fast?" she asked, when I set the box in her hand.

"I'm not the blind one here."

She fumbled to open it, finally revealing the delicate diamond ring tarnished with age. "It was Granny's," she said.

Without her able to stop me, I reached into the satin nest, pinched out the jewel, and slipped it onto the ring finger on my right hand, just as I had a hundred times before.

"I'm sure it's too big for you."

"It's not." I waggled my finger so she could see. "Can I have it?" I asked. "Please?"

My mother paused and tugged on the ring, expecting it to slide off. When it didn't, I saw her disappointment. She scrunched up her face and studied my hand. She seemed to be looking for a reason not to give it to me. "I don't know, Sandy," she said. "What are you going to do with it?"

"I'm going to wear it, of course."

She shut the drawer and brusquely plunked the velvet box in my hand. "You can have it," she said. "Just don't lose it. It's a treasure. A real one."

I looked her in the eye, so she could see my gratitude. "I know, Ma," I said. "Thank you. Really, thank you." Then, quietly giddy, I ducked out of the room before she could change her mind and take it back.

I went into my own room where I pulled up the white vinyl window shade and then sat on the edge of my bed, staring out at the familiar view. The neighborhood had that weak suburban glow of streetlamps and porch lights with eerie patches of dark, like mortar, between each house. Trees, mere saplings forty-something years ago when my father planted them, had grown past the height of our roof. And the blue spruce that I had once imagined we'd slide down if the bakery murderers came to kill us had been chopped down to use as our Christmas tree the last year my father was alive. That was 1984, the same year my grandmother died.

I studied her ring, so small and simple, a treasure indeed. I also heard a voice in my head. *Would you trade this ring for the chest of gold?* My son loved the game we called *Would you?* Usually it involved some random death-defying feat or unreasonable physical challenge in exchange for an exorbitant sum of money.

"Hey, Mom. Would you run up and down Mount Washington in a bathing suit for a million dollars?"

"Sure, if I could. But I don't think I could. Still, I'd definitely try."

"Would you eat ten pounds of raw meat? Actually, no, twenty pounds?"

Just to amuse him, I pretended to throw up in my mouth. "For a million dollars?"

"No, two million. But without stopping and nothing to wash it down, like no water."

"Hmm. I'd have to know what kind of meat it was first."

"Chicken."

As I thought about that, I actually felt the contents of my stomach rise in my throat. "No. Not chicken, but I'd try beef."

I slipped off the ring and held it tightly in my fist. I imagined pitching it into the darkness in exchange for secrets. What *would* I trade for the answer to where the treasure chest was hidden, or for what kept my mother so hidden from me? What did I trade for my life in Japan and later in Luxembourg? What was on the line now? Every quest requires a sacrifice. We must always give up something when we set off to search. Maybe those years overseas required me to disconnect from my mother, but perhaps this ring symbolized a chance at real engagement. Did my mother suddenly find me worthy? Was she ready to reconcile our differences and make a fumbling commitment to being closer? Or, was the offering more perfunctory than that? With life closing like a curtain over a window at dusk, did she feel the pressure to distribute her treasures? I only knew that she had shown it to me for reason, and I asked for it without apology or compunction. Maybe it was time for me to ask for more.

I slipped the ring back on my finger. I wouldn't trade it for anything.

35 - PAGES

My sister handed me *The All Service Polyglot Diary* with so little ceremony that I struggled at first to believe it was real. I immediately recognized the blue cardboard cover I had last seen in the attic almost four decades earlier. I turned the slender book around in my hands and then brought it to my nose for a whiff of mothballs.

It was summer, and Betsy was visiting from Munich for two weeks. My mother needed a pacemaker, and we'd been taking care of her tag-team style.

"Where on earth did you get this?" My voice came from outside my body.

"In my dresser," Betsy said. "I opened the top drawer, and it was just sitting there. I couldn't wait to show you."

"But the fish moths?" I stammered. "She said she got rid of it. So what the hell?"

"I know," Betsy said. "What the hell?"

Here it was. Not gone at all. My mother must have been hiding it, waiting for the right moment to release it to my sister in her usual way of doing things, on her terms, with no explanation. It didn't surprise me that she left it for Betsy to find, knowing how I ached for that book. It was my mother's way of exerting control over me, of not capitulating to my longing while rewarding Betsy for being less pushy.

But none of that mattered. I had the diary at last.

"Have you read it?" I asked Betsy.

"I only had time to skim through a few pages, but you go ahead."

Most unbelievably, the date was August first, what would have been my father's ninety-second birthday.

I took the book to the window seat in Mark's study overlooking the park and cracked open the dry binding, studying it for those fish moths. Finding no suspicious bugs, I smelled the pages again and smiled. Then I opened my heart as empty as a bucket, as if putting it out to catch rain after a drought. I had wanted to have the book with me, to go where my young father went, to see what he saw. I had so little of him. All these years, I just held tight to a few untarnished memories.

The pages detailed his experiences stationed in the Philippines in the summer of 1945. In his elegant slant, he wrote of long days playing bridge, making test flights, and flying soldiers to the island of Okinawa. He wrote about the letters he had received from his family, and some from that woman Della. Della in the diary.

The stories came back to me, connecting the small broken memories I had carried inside for so long, like the part about Della. Is that why my mother had kept the diary from me all those years? To protect me from the knowledge of a girlfriend that my father wrote to during World War II? Maybe, but, as I sat in the bright August light reading every word on every timeworn page, I could find nothing incriminating, nothing that could justify my mother's refusal to let me see the book when I wanted it. And maybe nothing was plenty. What do we hold back from our children? What do we leave out of our stories? Isn't there always something we can't reveal? Or won't?

Was it possible that by withholding this diary, my mother unwittingly set me off on my quest for my father, a lieutenant in the Army Air Corp, who diligently served his country, went to church on the base, longed for his mother's cooking and letters with news from home? Here he was again, the young father I had searched for all over the world. We had found each other at last.

That day, my father's diary gave me something Japan never quite did, the joy of becoming reacquainted with that boy-man who was yanked from his youth, away from his family and his sweetheart. More importantly, perhaps, I learned something about my father from what I *didn't* find in those pages. He never wrote about the horrors of war when he flew into battle or the evils that he, an innocent young man, must have witnessed and endured. Did he lose comrades he loved? See people die? What did he lose of himself that he could never talk about? What was it that silenced him to me?

When I finished reading the entire diary through, feeling my father's thudding young heart on every page, I turned back to August 1, 1945, my father's birthday.

Big day today. I am now a big grown boy of twenty-five, look ninety, so they tell me, and wish I was eight.

I bolted downstairs and started digging through my closet. I reached into a beat-up box in the back and pulled out my own diary from the day I turned twenty-five in Japan. October 29, 1989.

I sit here in my Tokyo apartment and still can't believe I got myself to this country. Did Daddy do this? Did he make this happen? Sometimes I wish I were a girl again, and he was still alive.

Through the years, I must have wished 1,000 wishes for my father and me to find each other. But this one—both of us in Japan at age twenty-five, yearning for something lost in our youth—just came true without my ever asking.

I set the two diaries on my writing desk, like tiny windows carved in the wall that had once come between my father and me.

36 - WAIT

"You need a night out," my friend Lisa insisted. We had met in a writing program that started on my first week in Boston and liked each other instantly. "You're not going to stay home and work on a Friday night, are you?"

I hesitated. This was the summer of 1994, and I had been writing diligently every day since returning to the States three weeks earlier. I was subletting my friend Paul's studio apartment on the edge of Boston's increasingly gentrified South End and really did need to get out more. With Paul away for the month, Lisa was my only friend in town.

We met at an Irish pub on Beacon Street in Brookline, where we were joined by Justine, a friend of hers from Brookline Booksmith, where they both worked. Lisa, a twenty-four-year-old redhead with pale Irish skin, was proving herself to be one of the best writers in our program. Justine was a model-thin, twenty-something with ink-black hair cut in a stunning pixie style, and a DNA double-helix tattooed around her upper arm. As we all fell into easy conversation, I knew I had been right to come out.

I scanned the shelves, considering what I wanted to drink, when my eyes landed on Freixenet, that matte black bottle of cheap champagne that I'd drunk with *Who* when we met at my college all those years ago. I ordered a glass.

"Are you celebrating something?" Justine asked. She and Lisa had chosen draft beers. With its rough wood floors and rousing

Irish fiddle music blaring through the speakers, it was more that kind of place.

"I don't know," I said. "Maybe my new life in Boston."

"So at least order the good stuff," she chided.

I laughed. "Freixenet reminds me of someone."

Lisa groaned. "Tell me you're not missing the Swedish guy already?"

"No. Europeans would never drink this cheap stuff. Someone else from years ago."

"Who is he?" Lisa asked.

"A guy from college," I said. "We haven't been in touch in years. He's probably married or, I don't know, cheating on his girlfriend, or maybe gay."

"Gay? Really?" Justine said. She delicately sipped at the foam on her beer.

"No. Not gay," I said, remembering those passionate nights in Brooklyn. "Definitely not gay."

Justine eyed Lisa. "She still likes him."

Lisa rolled her eyes. "Obviously."

"No," I said a little too insistently. "But something about living in the city this summer reminds me of him." Only then did I realize how powerfully those two brief nights in Brooklyn had imprinted on my memory. Ten years and three continents later, I was still thinking of him, of *Who*.

"Sandra just broke off an engagement," Lisa explained.

"Why?" Justine asked. I looked at her. It was so easy for women to open up to strangers.

"It just felt wrong," I said. "And if I'm committing to someone for the rest of my life, it had better feel really right. And passionate."

"Still, it was probably hard to leave?"

"Excruciating. But, in some ways, it was harder to build my life around a lie. What about you?" I asked her. "Are you in love?"

Justine smiled into her glass, her thin shoulders folding in. "I have a crush on my psychologist."

"Aren't therapists pretty much off-limits?" I asked.

"Kind of. Plus, I think he has a girlfriend. No ring though, so he's probably not married."

"How old is he?" Lisa asked.

She looked at us and scrunched up her face. "Late twenties maybe. I don't know much about him. He does this Freudian thing where he doesn't talk about himself."

"Does it work?" I asked.

"I guess so. I think I'm getting better."

"It's funny," I said, "the guy who dumped me." I held up my glass of Freixenet. "This one. He was studying to be a psychologist, too, first at Yale, and then at the University of Vermont for his doctorate."

Justine's head almost snapped when she turned to me. Her eyes got wide, then squinty. Her head tilted slightly, and a disbelieving smile pulled up the corner of her mouth. And I knew. I just knew, even before she spoke again, her voice incredulous.

"Was his name Mark?"

37 - HEART

While I leaned across his counter drinking a home-brewed lemon coriander beer, Mark sautéed onions for the vegetarian pizza he was making. After connecting with me in the bar the week before, Justine brought a note I'd written with my phone number into her next therapy session. Minutes after their session ended, Mark called and invited me to his place for dinner that Friday.

"Can I help?" I asked, watching him try to gather ingredients with one hand as he stirred with the other.

"Want to crush some garlic?"

With a blunt paring knife, I nicked the ends off of five cloves and, one by one, set them into the well of the press, crushing until the pungency mixed with the aroma of caramelized onions, the sizzle and steam almost lyrical as it drifted up from the cast-iron pan. As Mark tossed a handful of cornmeal across the pizza stone, I recognized his long, artistic fingers, and the quick, sure movements of his wrist when he stretched the dough over his fists.

But what stays with me from that night, more indelibly than the cooking and conversation, is how he looked when he came to the door to pick me up, the familiarity of that boy I met when we were both nineteen, the one I called *Who*. He looked mostly the same, just ever so slightly gentled by age. His face was a little fuller, his hair a bit tamer, his almond-shaped eyes less searching—more settled on what was in front of him. When I saw him, I had only one thought: *Here he is.*

While inspecting his kitchen shelf, I also recognized the worn paperback copy of *The Joy of Cooking*, the very book I had given him a decade before when I visited him in Brooklyn.

I pointed at it. "Is that . . . ?

"Yep. Still use it."

Biting my lip and looking around, I could tell that this moment held my life, the way one drop of water contains the sea. I wasn't lurching forward into the future or leaning back into my past; rather, I was standing squarely in my body with a clear sense that every clue had led me right here into this ugly yellow Boston kitchen (not unlike Mark's ugly yellow Brooklyn kitchen), where he was making me pizza on a hot summer night. For the first time in years, I wasn't aching to be anywhere else.

What did we talk about? We started with our lives over the last decade. While I was living abroad, he was getting his Ph.D. in Vermont, and had recently launched his clinical practice at a prestigious psychiatric hospital. He had traveled a bit but, having recently finished graduate school, didn't have much money to blow. I told him of Europe, of teaching, and of travel, and how so many of my dreams had come true in the most surprising of ways.

Summer had descended on Boston like a pressed hand; you either took refuge in the air-conditioning or embraced the weather New Englanders knew so well but still vociferously groaned about. With the pizza in the oven, Mark's apartment was turning into a sweat lodge, so we took our beers to his screened-in porch. We settled into two low blue chairs, the only place to sit down, except on a hideous gold bouclé sofa (inherited from a favorite aunt, he explained).

"Most of the furniture we had was Janice's," he said, referring to his girlfriend of four years. They'd broken up amicably on the same day that I'd left my boyfriend in Luxembourg. "I bought these chairs today. What do you think?"

"You bought them today?"

"On my way home from work. I didn't want to invite you over to sit on the floor." He glimpsed across the living room. "Or on that sofa."

"Thank you for sparing me that." It was so deliciously easy to tease him. "You went out and bought chairs for our date? And ten years ago in Brooklyn you wouldn't even walk me to the subway station."

He winced a bit and scooted his blue chair around to face mine. "You know," he began, "for years I've wanted to apologize for how I acted back then."

"Please," I said, holding up my palm. "That just came out. It's nothing I've dwelled on."

"Even so." He cocked his head at me. I wasn't sure what to expect. "I always liked you," he said. "I liked you so much. But there was always distance between us, or about to be, and I'm not good at distance. I knew even then there is nothing about long-distance relationships that appeals to me. So instead I acted like a jerk. And I'm truly sorry."

I smiled as I breathed in his apology. It changed the air, diffused something that I perhaps hadn't even realized I'd brought to the date, a chewed-over idea that he was very sexy and fun but maybe not completely kind. "Thank you," I said. Then I studied him and, just like that, felt ten years wash away. Ten years that weren't there anymore. Ten years that held so much—our twenties, our growth into adulthood, other lovers that made us better people and moved our lives to different places—this place, in these new blue chairs, facing each other.

As if reading my mind, Mark said, "Janice taught me a lot about being in a relationship. She's a smart feminist. She didn't take shit from me."

"I can tell," I said, in deep appreciation of the sisterhood of women who make our men better. "She humbled you."

"She did indeed." When he smiled at me, I suddenly

remembered how one tooth crossed slightly over the other in a small collision of bone.

Mark and I stared at each other for a few seconds, neither of us saying what we knew might be true—fate was having a field day with us, putting us together at this point in our lives, both recently single, both finally ready for this. We might have kept on staring, if it weren't for the smoke of the burning pizza wafting through three rooms to reach the sunporch. We rushed to the kitchen where Mark fumbled with the unwieldy pizza stone before dropping it onto the stove in a clamor of metal.

"See. This is what you get when you apologize," I said. The kitchen was a haze of gray. Burning crisps of cornmeal ringed the blackened crust.

"Yeah. That'll teach me. Never again," he said, tossing down the oven mitt. "No more apologies ever." He tried chipping off pieces of the burnt crust with a spatula, salvaging what he could. "You know?" he said, turning to me and smiling broadly. "This chance was worth a lot of burnt pizzas."

Out on the porch again, tucked into our chairs, we toasted to second chances, to fate, to our exes, to ten years apart, to the summer ahead. We talked long past dark, recalling the night we danced over the Brooklyn Bridge into Manhattan, our romp on Brighton Beach, and the twenty-five dollar bottles of Trefethen we drank with friends in a Greenwich Village wine bar in our college days. We talked and talked, and there was still so much to say, but we were both bleary-eyed from alcohol and the heat and sharing a decade's worth of stories.

"Since I've had a few beers, I should wait a while before driving you home," Mark said when he caught me yawning. "But I can call you a cab. Or—"

"Or?"

"You're welcome to stay here. I do have air-conditioning upstairs."

"Maybe I should just take a cab."

"That's fine. But didn't you say your sublet has no air-conditioning?"

"I don't mind. Well, not that much. I mean it is pretty hot."

"I really need air-conditioning on a night like this."

"I also don't have any of my things with me."

"Well, if you stayed, I could lend you a T-shirt, or boxers."

"Not both?"

"Or both, although I'd be fine with one or the other. Less laundry." He smiled. "Oh and Janice took the bed. But I have a double mattress on the floor. So, you decide."

"I have to decide?"

"Yes," he said, nodding. "You do."

"How about this," I said. "You take me upstairs, and I'll see how that air-conditioning feels. *Then* I'll decide."

"Sounds like a plan. Follow me."

I did. The room felt good, but Mark felt better. In fact, he felt so good that I never left.

Two summers later, Mark and I proposed to each other with treasures we found on a red sand beach on Prince Edward Island where we were vacationing. I gave him a perfectly preserved dried crab the size of my thumbnail and half a clamshell, the color of ivory. Mark had found a tiny sand dollar and a silvery-blue mussel shell. We exchanged them on the beach as if they were precious jewels. That night, celebrating our engagement at a restaurant near our cottage, we asked the waitress for their best champagne.

"We only have one kind," she told us and brought out a bottle of Freixenet.

Mark choked on a sip of water. "Even I know a sign when I see one," he said.

The following August, dear Liz, my minister roommate who had been there for me at every juncture, married us on the grounds of an old stone castle overlooking the Atlantic. My mother walked me down the grass aisle. Betsy stood beside me as my maid of honor. A friend sang "Amazing Grace," my father's favorite hymn, and a photo of my mother shows her dabbing her eyes as she listened. Finally, Lisa told our love story to the crowd of family and friends who had traveled from three continents to be with us on that late summer day. "Everyone you are afraid you have lost," she whispered, "may be secretly waiting in a hidden corner for the right moment to come back to you."

38 - SUPERSTORM

When I woke on October 29, 2012, the morning of my forty-eighth birthday, school had already been canceled for Phinny and Addie, and the East Coast was hunkering down, awaiting the arrival of the storm of the century. Superstorm Sandy. How could I not feel oddly and personally connected to the storm when on this day in 1964, in a factory town in Connecticut, a few dozen people awaited my arrival? After my mother labored under strong drugs, as was the norm in those days, I was born at 5:15 in the evening, small and healthy, but always, according to my mother, a force of nature.

In some ways, I left the name Sandy behind when I began publishing with the byline Sandra A. Miller (a more distinguished moniker, I believed); in other ways, my childhood nickname, Sandy (Sandra's spunkier younger sister), like the beach it conjured, never left me. It's what my family still called me and the name that best identified my gritty, ocean-loving soul.

Sandy. I must have heard the name one hundred times that day. Sandy. Sandy. Superstorm Sandy. What was my birthday hurricane going to do? What path would she choose?

39 - UNCOVERED

With Thanksgiving just three days and many cooking hours away, I was heading to bed at 10 p.m. when I heard the home phone downstairs.

I don't like phones ringing after 9:30 at night, my cut-off time for nonemergency calls. After 9:30 p.m. is open season for disasters and death.

Mark hurried to answer while I strained to listen from the second floor.

"Oh, hey, David," he said.

David. 10 p.m. A weeknight.

"Who found it?" I shouted. In just my T-shirt and underwear, I bolted down the stairs. The house had that late November chill when the cold just muscles its way inside you; I was shivering when I grabbed the phone from Mark's hand.

"Who?" I panted at David. "When?"

"The pirate guys dug it up themselves," David said in his ever-calm voice. "It's in the *New York Times*. The on-the-ground clues were wrecked by Hurricane Sandy, and I imagine saltwater was starting to corrode the coins."

"So, you mean, Hurricane Sandy found it? On *my* birthday?"

"Yep! And they donated the money to Hurricane Relief. But are you ready for this?"

I knew from the hook in his voice. He was going to say how close we'd come.

I was right. He did. We did. The treasure had been buried in Floyd Bennett Field, that ghost airport in Brooklyn where we spent two long spring days searching, but not finding. It was in the very first place we went, and the place where we wrongly decided it wasn't.

"Dammit," I said. "Goddammit!" With David still on the phone, I dashed to my office and turned on the computer. A quick Google search gave me the link to a *New York Times* blog piece. I started skimming until I got to this part: "... *the North 40 Natural Area, part of the Gateway National Recreation Area.*"

"The North Forty!" I shouted. "NO!"

"Is that what it says?" David asked. "I'd only glanced at the story when I called you."

"Yep." I began reading out loud. *"It was next to Floyd Bennett Field in southeast Brooklyn, not more than 300 yards from a parking lot . . . ."*

"That's where we went that day with the carnival. That was the parking lot—"

"We had to pass the police barricades, the Jersey barriers—"

"And the No Trespassing Sign—"

"It was probably blocked that day only because of the carnival."

"And any other day we would have had access. But remember it was pitch dark and then the police car came?"

The photo showed the two pirate puppeteers who created the search, Damien and Vincent, digging up our treasure chest from a deep dirt hole. I sat back in my office chair and quietly read the rest of the story while David did the same.

Throughout the two years of our searching, I would often whisper these words to myself, as if I were telling the story of my life: *Sandy unearths the treasure.* And on my birthday, *Hurricane* Sandy did sort of unearth the treasure. I should have specified exactly which Sandy I meant. Me. *This* Sandy. *Not* the hurricane.

"The North Forty!" I said to David when I was done reading.

"We were probably twenty yards away. If we had just kept walking that day."

If.

"Is it a relief that it's been found?" Mark asked when I crawled into bed that night. I curled into him, grateful for his body heat.

"I thought it would be," I said. "But mostly I feel this loss, like all of a sudden I'm in a state of mourning."

"Of course. You invested so much in that treasure hunt."

"I mean, in a way, I'm happy the puppeteers dug it up and that we weren't just outwitted by some nerdy code guys from Schenectady or something. That would have killed me."

"Schenectady? That's a funny name, isn't it?"

"And it's nice about the charity."

"Mmm."

"You know, every day for two years I thought about that treasure, if only in some peripheral way. At first it was all about obsession, but then it mutated into something more like reassurance. However crappy a day it had been, I knew that somewhere out there in New York City was this chest of gold waiting to be found. As long as it remained unfound, I could let myself feel hopeful."

Mark bunched up the pillow and readjusted his head. "I'm listening."

"There's just something," I said, "about trekking around the hidden corners of New York City with a shovel in your hand and this belief that you might dig up gold. Something that raises a day out of the ordinary."

"I get that," he murmured. I could feel him trying hard to listen, fighting sleep.

"It was a reminder," I said, "that something was out there for me, maybe something that I had been searching for my entire life. Not treasure, exactly, but something. I never told you this, but on that first day in Brooklyn, I stood alone in the middle of Floyd Bennett Field and kept saying, *Where? Where is it?* Without really knowing what I've been looking for, I've been on an even bigger treasure hunt for these past two years. Did you realize that?"

I felt the heaviness of Mark's arm on my pelvis and took it in my hands. As always, since the day my mother gave it to me, I was wearing my grandmother's gold ring. I kissed Mark's knuckles and rubbed them against my cheek.

"What?" he asked, briefly pulling back from the edge of sleep.

"That's okay," I told him. "You don't need to understand. It was personal."

40 - GRATITUDE

"What's new?" my mother asked. Out for lunch in New Britain, we were waiting for our small pizza and house salads to arrive.

"The treasure was dug up a few days ago," I told her. "You know that chest of gold coins I was trying to find in New York?"

She put down a half-eaten roll and looked at me. "What?" Her mouth, still full of partially chewed bread, hung open. "Who found it?"

"The flooding from Hurricane Sandy messed up the area and the clues. So the guys who buried it dug it up."

"Now, what are you saying? They dug it up?" She fiddled with her hearing aid until it emitted a high-pitched beep.

"They dug up the ten thousand dollars and donated the money to Hurricane Relief."

"Well, isn't that something?"

"It bummed me out."

"Why?"

"My friend David and I wanted to find it."

"Oh!" She laughed until she snorted. "I guess you'll have to look harder next time." She took another big bite of her roll, and as I watched her chew, I felt something break inside me. I couldn't pretend anymore.

On our way home, we rode in near silence. But approaching our driveway, my mother said, "I worry about Betsy. Is she okay?"

"I think so," I said. I Skyped with my sister every weekend and saw her family on their summer visits, during which Betsy, racked with guilt for living so far away in Munich, did everything possible to make up for it. "She's always sacrificing for people," I said, and, if there are scraps of time left over, she maybe takes a few for herself, and then apologizes for it."

"Well, that's how Betsy has always been."

I swallowed hard, unable to resist this opening. I made an effort to lighten my tone, pitching my voice up an octave, out of those minor chords of accusation that tended to get me in trouble. "Is that why you always liked her better?" I asked. My question didn't quite have the note of levity I was trying for, but then again, when do such words ever land lightly?

"Well," my mother responded, "I wouldn't say that, exactly." She dove a hand into her purse and began rifling through random compartments, ripping open the zippers without finding anything, probably because she wasn't looking for anything. Finally, she sat up and sighed. "Betsy was just easier."

I took my time pulling into the driveway. With the car still moving, she grabbed for the door handle, but her purse spilled off her lap and onto the floor. "What the heck?" She gathered up the contents in a congested bundle and pushed open the door. She was trying to swing her legs out when I finally came to a full stop.

"You know . . ." I said, hesitantly, "I always feel like I've disappointed you."

She tried to slide out of the car. "Cripes, Sandy. Why would you even say such a thing?"

"Because that's how I feel, like you don't even care enough to get to know me, and never have."

I waited, anticipating her shutdown tactics. She would accuse me of being ridiculous, and then laugh at me with a sneer hovering on her lips. In healthier times she would have darted to the Wawa, lighting a cigarette before she was out of the driveway. But, without an escape plan, all she could do that day was tap her foot around in the air and try to make contact with solid ground.

"Daddy, too," I continued, because my switch had flipped to autopilot. "I never felt like he knew me. We never had a real relationship."

"Well, Sandy, you were very tough."

Tears blurred my eyes until I couldn't see clearly. "Maybe Daddy was the tough one," I said. "Sometimes I think that maybe his father was abusive to him."

"What do you mean abusive? What are you talking about?"

"How else did he get that way? Maybe from the war when he had to be tough? I'm just speculating, but something must have happened to him."

She waved me off. "I'm not buying this. I see these people on television talking about how things *happened* to them and that's why they are the way they are, and personally I think that's just a crock."

I wanted to laugh or maybe give her a shove, but she looked so frail sitting there that I think I could have toppled her with a strong exhale.

"I'm not accusing Daddy of anything," I said. "I'm just saying *he* was tough. I was always afraid of him, and then he died. Do you know how it felt at his funeral to have those people come up to me saying how much they loved him and telling all those stories about the things they'd done with him? I was jealous because he was *my* father, and I didn't even know him! Sometimes I wondered if he even loved me."

"Sandy, where on earth do you come up with these things?"

"From a lifetime of wondering about them. That's where."

"A lifetime? That's what you've been doing your whole life? Wondering if anyone loved you?"

"Not anyone. Daddy." I paused. "And in a way, you. Yes. That's a lot of what I've been doing."

She managed to get out of the car and close the door. I jumped out from my side and ran around to get her. It would stink to have her fall and die at that point, especially if I could prevent it.

I followed her to the house where she wriggled the key into the lock, threw open the door, and shuffled to the counter behind her gray wall. As she stared out the window, I stood back and studied her profile, the sag of her jowls, the large nose and platinum hair.

"And with you," I said after a moment, "I feel like you don't want anything to do with us. You don't have a relationship with my kids. And I can't bear to hear one more time about how great all of your friends' grandkids are or how you went to this one's soccer game or that one's recital. My heart breaks on every birthday, every Christmas, every Easter that you find a reason *not* to visit us. My heart just fucking breaks." My face was soaked with tears that I didn't wipe away.

My mother pursed her lips and lifted her chin. Then, after the longest moment, when I thought she might actually say something kind—I always thought she might actually say something kind, because hoping around her was one of my great downfalls—she looked down at her pink sweatshirt. "Cripes," she said when her eyes landed on a stain the circumference of a pea. "This shirt is an absolute mess." When she tried to take it off, her arms got tangled in the sleeves. I helped pull it over her head until she was standing there in her white T-shirt—just old bones and hanging flesh. I stepped aside to where she couldn't see me and wiped her not-stained pink sweatshirt across my face. It smelled like her laundry detergent and Nivea.

"Give me that," she said. She turned and tried to grab the clump from my hands. "If I don't get that stain out right now, it's going to be ruined."

"No," I said, not letting go.

"No?"

"Tell me something first. One nice thing." I didn't say it, but I thought it: *Give me something I can store away for when you're gone.*

"I don't know what you want me to tell you, Sandy. This whole conversation seems pretty ridiculous." When she reached for the shirt again, I pulled it back.

"Tell me that I didn't disappoint you," I said.

"Now, Sandy, what is this all about?"

"Can you just say it?"

"What? That I'm not disappointed in you?"

"Yes."

"Of course I'm not." She tore a paper towel from the roll and balled it in her fist. Then she started wiping down the immaculately clean stovetop. "I can't believe all of the things you manage to do."

"Like what?"

"I don't know. All those things. I don't know how you have the energy for them."

My breathing slowed. I lowered the shirt. "Tell me."

"Well, you write articles, and you do volunteer work, and you teach. You've lived all over the place. You amaze me sometimes."

"I amaze you?"

"Sometimes."

"Really?" I fell against the gray wall, taking in the full weight of her words. *You amaze me sometimes.* As always, I was wearing the ring she had given me, a physical symbol that I believed connected us. But this—this was real connection. It was just one sentence, but it felt heavy and true.

"Thank you," I whispered.

"You're welcome. Now give me that shirt so I can wash it."

41 - LOST

On a sunny Friday in June, I was hustling to heat up some left-over soup for breakfast when I stopped short at the ringing phone. I glanced at the caller ID: *Charles Young*. My uncle. I knew.

I knew with such unwavering certainty that I couldn't even pick the phone up and answer. Instead, with trembling hands, I set down the soup bowl as the machine went to message. Then I listened as my Aunt Mary's voice, desperate and high-pitched, filled the kitchen.

"Sandy, I need to talk to you. Are you there?"

Her frantic tone confirmed my instinct, but as long as I didn't touch that phone, as long as she didn't say the words out loud, it wasn't real. "I'll try your cell phone," Mary said, and hung up fast.

My face squeezed shut. The world felt so dark. Did I shout *No!* out loud? The moment seared with such hard-burning pain that I momentarily lost connection to reality.

When my cell phone rang seconds later, I acted as if I hadn't heard the first message. In that way, I kept my mother alive a little longer. I had a chance to pause in the space between life and death, before . . . before what? Everlasting grief? Relief? I didn't know. For the hundreds of times I had imagined this moment, it appeared that day as a stranger.

After hanging up with Mary, I paced from the kitchen to the living room, back down the hallway, and then into the family room where I collapsed on the floor, doubling into myself—wailing—or maybe the word is *keening*. The pain came in waves, not low and stabbing as in childbirth, but high up in the heart so that I cried aloud with each one. The world never seemed more blank, like a chalkboard wiped down to a few gray smears, the particles of dust floating in the space between what was and what will be no more.

"What's up?" Mark asked when I called him. "I'm about to start a session."

"My mother died."

His gasp made it real. I fell onto the couch where I stayed, hardly moving, until Mark arrived at my side fifteen minutes later.

Next, I called Betsy and we cried together in that shared fog of disbelief.

Then I got in the car and drove like the wind. I needed to see my mother. I needed to see her lying in her bedroom because I hadn't seen my father, because his death had been held beyond my reach, sending me on a search around the world for clues that would solve the puzzle of his passing from life, his and mine. Everything would be different this time, I thought, as I barreled down the Mass Pike, with a line from a Pablo Neruda poem washing through me like breath: "Tonight I can write the saddest lines."

As I drove, I called Liz and Paul and sobbed to them on the phone. I called my friend Marilyn, who lived a few miles from my mom and asked her to meet me at the house. When I got tired of crying, explaining, and accepting condolences, I focused my eyes on the clear June sky and tried to see my mother. Was she reuniting with my father? Hugging her own mother? Maybe she was lighting up a cigarette and saying, "Cripes. I'm glad that's over with." I laughed at that image, but then laughing made me cry. Finally, I put on a Pavarotti CD that I'd taken from her house the month before and cried some more as I listened, over and over, to "La Donne È Mobile" from *Rigoletto*. How could one voice hold the world like that?

When I arrived at last at my mother's home of almost fifty years, I pushed the door open, just as I had thousands of times, anticipating a roast chicken waiting inside. Looking around, I saw she had set the coffee maker the night before. I flicked it on, grateful for this last offering.

Marilyn came from the living room and hugged me. She had already peeked into the bedroom (she had Mother Teresa's heart with the guts of a Navy Seal) and told me what to expect. "I just didn't want you to be shocked," she said gently. "You'll see her feet first."

"Feet first," I repeated. "Okay. Feet I can handle."

We tiptoed up the carpeted stairs, gripping each other like two teenage girlfriends gathering the courage to face a trapped mouse, the cute boy at the dance—a mother's dead body.

I saw her feet first, as promised. She was on the floor where the EMTs had laid her down in a routine attempt to revive her. As I took the last stair onto the second-floor landing, I could see her whole body on the floor, the pink blanket pulled up to her torso, her hands folded across her chest.

I fell on the floor for the second time that day and wept; Marilyn patted my back until I was ready. Finally I drew a breath and crawled closer. I had to see for myself. I had to understand this death. I had to walk myself almost systematically through disbelief and grief. I crawled to the threshold of her bedroom and stopped. "Her eyes are open," I said.

"How about I shut them?" Marilyn said.

I choked when I laughed.

"What's so funny?"

"Yes, Marilyn, please shut my dead mother's eyes."

Then Marilyn, dear Marilyn, tried her best, but she could only close them halfway.

"In the movies they put quarters on them," I said.

"Let's not do that."

"No," I agreed. "Let's not."

My mother was wearing a white T-shirt with a short pink ter-rycloth bathrobe and two pink sponge curlers in her hair. Had she planned to sleep in that bathrobe? I wondered. Maybe it happened early in the evening while she was watching *Jeopardy*. I loved the idea of death as final *Jeopardy*. A small tube where the EMT had tried to resuscitate her still hung between her lips, reminding me of the ubiquitous cigarettes. She wore a silver necklace tight at her throat and two silver rings, likely bought at T.J. Maxx: one a plain band, one with a Kokopelli dancer. Her mouth was slack.

So that was it, I thought. She set the coffee pot, took out her teeth, put in her curlers, and never woke up. That is a damn good death.

Even several hours dead, she still looked exactly as she looked each night before bed, only now so completely drained of life that I struggled to internalize this finality, to cross the threshold to acceptance. It made no sense. Somehow I had been operating on the false belief that death couldn't catch this woman who, even in pain and old age and sleep, found a way to be in motion. My mother had performed such mindboggling feats of movement and escape in life that I assumed she could pretend in death, as well. I simply didn't believe she would ever look like this. Dead. So very dead.

Marilyn and I kneeled beside her and said the Our Father.

"How about a Hail Mary, too," Marilyn suggested. And we did.

Then I cried from a wellspring that I once thought was shal-low. I cried for myself, clutching Marilyn with wracking sobs, exactly as my mother would never have allowed, eliciting the most visceral pain, the kind my mother had no tolerance for. Only this time she couldn't stop me. That's how powerful death was; it had banished her ability to tell me not to feel. It had freed me to be in that house, fully aware of my loss and not set that loss aside, not take it to lunch, not bury it in fear. In stilling the frantic hand of control my mother held over everything she touched in life, this pale-pink death of hers had finally set me free.

When it was time to call the undertaker, I grasped for a way to stay longer.

"I'll be right down the hall," Marilyn said, tiptoeing out of the room.

I looked again at my mother, no longer my mother, but always my mother. "Do you have any idea how much I miss you already?" I said to her. "Do you? Do you have any idea? Do you know that I want to talk to you right now? That I've never in my life wanted to talk to you so badly?"

It was simply mind-blowing that she didn't talk back. It still felt more like a magic trick that she would wake up from than an actual end. So I kept going. Talking. Telling her things, whatever popped into my head. "It's fine. It's okay. We'll be okay. It's Friday, you know? A beautiful spring day. A real Betty day, if ever there was one." I could have sat next to her all afternoon, talking non-sense, prolonging the moment of leaving, asking her questions I'd never have the answers to. But in the end, I was more ready than I thought. And so I did it. I took one last good look and leaned over my mother with her platinum poof and half-open blue eyes. I touched her hand, her cheek, the top of her blonde head, and then the quiet spot above her heart and said what at last, but not too late, felt deeply true.

"I love you, Ma."

42 - FOUND

The physical qualities of grief, expansive like vapor and resisting containment, blindsided me. That sense of missing my mother would begin in my gut, float up into my heart, and linger there before reaching my throat, almost choking me on its way to my tear ducts. It would wait, stinging my eyes until the tears let down, offering a moment's relief before the sadness struck again, more searing somehow, compounded by every remembrance.

With the funeral and wake behind us, Betsy and her family flew back to Germany. Phinny and Addie finished the school year and were soon distracted by the freedoms of summer, while Mark returned to the status quo of work, pausing to offer a steady hand when he found me stumbling around trying to navigate the rocky path of sorrow.

"I only want to talk to people with two dead parents," I explained one night, the two of us curled around each other in a corner of our unmade bed. "You know, other orphans."

"Well, I can't help with that, but let's find you some orphans then."

"I feel so resentful toward people who don't have any idea what this kind of grief is like."

"What's it like?" Mark asked. "Show me."

"It's like this," I said, turning to face him. My eyes were red and swollen; my cheeks burned hot from the tears. "It's stupid and mean, and it beats the crap out of you."

This is how grief led me back to Mark. We had never gone through loss together, not of someone close, but there it was, this death, creating an overlap of experience, a chance to sit together in our sadness, or share a meal and remember my mother. Also, with the great treasure hunt over, I stopped disappearing and rejoined the family. One night, about a month after my mom's passing, Phinny looked up from his dinner as if I had just been teleported to the table. "Wait a minute," he said. "Where the hell have you been, Mom?"

"Grandma Betty just died," Addie explained, as a way of excusing me. "She's been dealing with all of that stuff, Phinny."

"It's more than that," I assured my daughter. "But I'm back now."

"You'd better be," Mark said.

In bed that night, wrung out with exhaustion, Mark and I lay side-by-side, our fingers touching, too tired to grip. Since my mother's death, we'd hardly had a moment alone, and the heat of that summer night stirred something primal in us. "I'm really horny," I whispered, "but I'm too exhausted to do anything about it."

"I know," Mark agreed, his voice dropping. "I wish someone would just come in here and sex us."

I laughed so hard that I pulled a muscle in my chest. Then I rolled on top of my husband and kissed his mouth with a deep, remembered hunger.

The following night my mother appeared in my dream. She was trying to tell me something but couldn't speak. I sat up in a panic unable to remember the sound of her gravelly voice, and at 2:30 a.m., fully alert, dashed downstairs to the home answering machine and played back all fifty-one messages that hadn't been erased. There were three from her. The last one sent me to my knees. "Sandy. It's Mom. Now I got your latest newspaper article, and it's very nice . . ."

I would never hear anyone say that again: *Sandy. It's Mom.*

Sitting on the floor in the early morning hours, grief filled the space around and inside me, pressing on my chest, my stomach, my throat with dull insistence. But I couldn't pick it up and clutch it in my hand. I couldn't slip it into my pocket and finger the edges of my pain.

Rising to my hands and knees, but too bone-tired to stand up and walk, I crawled down the hardwood floor of the hallway and into my office, illuminated by the light of the summer moon filtered through the branches of our mulberry trees. Still kneeling, I reached into the recesses of my office closet and slid out eight boxes, including the five that I'd brought from my mother's house the week before. My trove.

Beginning with the forty-year-old Buster Brown shoebox secured with crumbling layers of tape, I removed the items, one by one, and began arranging them, not in a linear order, necessarily, but in a way that made sense to me.

I inserted a white shell between a pebble—the same blue-green color as the eyes of my grade-school crush—and the granite arrowhead found in the nearby woods. Then I placed a small filigree cross on top.

I pulled out the red lighter that once offered protection from the bakery murderers in our town; the lighter no longer worked—the fire of that fear had burned out long ago—but the curve of plastic in my palm brought back a remembered sense of safety.

From high school, there were bobby pins, a Barbie doll head that Paul once left in my car as a joke, a roach clip from a night hanging with the stoners, and a white button found after my senior prom in the way back of my boyfriend's VW van. I laid those side-by-side.

In my college boxes, I dug out the two Molson caps from the weekend Mark broke my heart at Liz's party on Long Island and a gold key chain discovered on the floor of an English Department classroom the day I won a writing award. In the Los Angeles box, I found warped coasters from nights with clients in Beverly Hills and a handful of gold and silver keys—all of them picked up around my apartment building downtown; with a little sleuthing, I probably could have broken into a good number of my neighbors' homes.

I spent hours on that floor arranging each item just so, while the moon outside my window slid to the western corner of the early summer sky, and, behind me, the sun rose in that first startling burst of light, like a switch had been thrown. I left no object unexamined, picking up each—a bouquet of plastic flowers, a pair of ink-black feathers, a broken cigarette snatched from my mother's purse that always smelled of tobacco, and Tic Tacs.

In my Tokyo box I had dozens of flattened origami animals left behind in classrooms and dozens of cotton handkerchiefs, a reminder that I had made lifelong friends in the same country where my father had gone to war.

Through these mementos I could still touch the struggle of a heart that refused to stay with the wrong men, the gamble of moving to unknown cities, and then the jackpot of Mark, then Phinny, then Addie. The three of them appeared in so many of the bits and pieces that made up my Boston life. They were in shiny pennies and waxy Bazooka gum cartoons, and a seamless brown chestnut marked with nature's light brown fingerprint.

Scraps of my writing were everywhere, too, but never more obvious than the day, disheartened by an editor's blistering rejection, I decided to quit the creative life. I went outside to get away from my computer, and there in front of my house was a silvery gray shard of graphite. I had never seen natural graphite before, only the kind in pencils, and I just held it in my hand, disbelieving. Later I used it to scrawl in my journal. *Don't quit. Don't.*

I didn't stop sorting, arranging, and laying out more than forty years of found things, until I had emptied the very last box, my most recent trove. In it were some shards of glass that I found on the bike path late one night. Next to them I placed the piece of blue-and-white crockery discovered that first afternoon in Floyd Bennett Field, not far from where Hurricane Sandy revealed the chest of gold. I had known in my gut that it was the place. Choosing to ignore it, though, and to keep searching gave me other unexpected riches that I never would have discovered had the hunt stopped that day.

Then I sat and gazed at all of it. There were thousands of objects in front of me, appearing labyrinthine as they circled in paths, wound around my office floor, and meandered up and down, often spiking like an EKG reading when the heart beats too fast. Some items were forced together because they only made sense in partnership, while others required space, but every one of them was connected to the next, like pieces of a puzzle, revealing a startlingly clear picture of my life—expansive, nuanced, messy, full, wicked, silly, circuitous, and well lived. There was no way to look at my dozens of journals and get this bird's eye view of each moment in time and its relationship to the next, and the next. There was no other way to see myself at the center of my own collection of stories and clues and treasures as I did that day at dawn, with every one of my senses alert to the complexity of my wholeness. This was my path as I had walked it, my unambiguous path. If I'd been confused before, I understood now that every moment, however miniscule and seemingly meaningless, was essential to my arrival at this place.

Perhaps what I saw most clearly that early July morning was this: no matter what I found next, my journey would continue. Nothing could stop the momentum of my life.

It was light in my office when I scooped up handfuls of found things in no order at all and stuffed them back into the boxes, none of them fitting well as I jumbled them together. If I never looked at them again, that would be okay. I knew them all by heart.

I went back upstairs to where Mark was still asleep and curled up next to my beloved. His arms were heavy and warm as they found me in that narrow intersection of light and darkness, sleep and consciousness, grief and love—the safety of his embrace allowing me to glimpse something new. It came in a small flash that I chased, like a firefly, trying to catch understanding in the clear glass jar of my heart. What was it exactly?

A recognition? A knowing? A realization that we have each been given a set number of pulses in life, and they could cease at any moment? How little space exists between life and death. Just a heartbeat really. Then it's over. Our moment in time. And what matters then? Perhaps just one thing: the quality of our love.

Is it deep and abiding? Is it conscious? Is it felt? Is it bigger than our fear? Does it transcend pain? Is it open to forgiveness? Is it the best we can do?

As for my mother, who knows? We may have another life together with more chances to sit and chat over pizza and salad. I hope so. But in this lifetime, in the care packages she sent to Tokyo and the pastel T-shirts she mailed to Boston, her return address carefully lettered in black marker on each box, came a version of her love, the best she could do. All I can do now is wait for the jagged edges of pain to be smoothed over by time, like broken glass churned by the sea and worn into an opaque memory of its once sharp self.

I don't expect I'll change much. I'll still growl at my children now and then, and huff at Mark in my low moments. When I feel empty, I'll still wander down the bike path, swiping my eyes over the asphalt in some habitual search for answers, and I'll still gaze up into the trees looking for a crow with a stone in her beak. Someday, if we happen to find each other, I'll thank her for trying to save me that day. At the same time, I'll make every effort to live inside my life, remembering to crawl into each small moment and have a good look around.

And when you do that, Sandy, I tell myself, *you'll see that forgiveness stops being hard, and joy becomes the default. Laughter outbids tears, and gold can be found, not in a father's diary, a mother's dresser drawer, endless stretches of beach, or some open field in New York City, but close enough that you can reach it just by lifting a hand to your heart and recognizing what's inside: the stories from your journey that have brought you to this place. Whether they were easy or tough, brutal or beautiful, it doesn't matter anymore. The alchemy of love has transformed them into gold, a sun-bright radiance that is yours to light the darkness.*

The hunt is over. You have found it. It was here all along inside each heartbeat, just waiting for you to notice. Made of breath and love and endless longing for the world, quite simply, you are the treasure.

→ END ←

Acknowledgments

At some point in the writing process, I realized that everyone I have ever been close to has contributed to this memoir, unwittingly or not. Although I can't thank all of you here, please know that you have enriched my life and words in immeasurable ways, and *Trove* would most certainly be a different book if we hadn't ever met.

As for the specific experience of bringing this story into the world, my heart beats with gratitude for those who have been essential to this creative journey in a more deliberate way.

Thank you to my publisher, Wendy Thomas Russell, for your warmth, intuition, and sharply focused editorial vision. You and your team have been fantastic to work with, and I'm wildly grateful that I landed on the welcoming shores of Brown Paper Press.

I am forever indebted to my dear friends and patient readers who offered ideas, edits and buoying words as I struggled to tell this story: John Adams, Sara Backer, Jeanine Brennan, Catherine Carney, Erin Copeland, Susan Curtin, Synthia Demetriou, Deb Fleischman, Stephanie Fox, Tim Grace, Liz Grabiner, Kathy Hallissey, Kelley Hurley, Paul Januszewski, Liz Junod, Kate Kapstad, Susan Keane, Nicola Kemmler, Marjorie Leary, Michelle Lemp, Steve Maas, Ellen Miller, Gary Miller, Margaret Moody, Steve Morgan, DeAnn O'Donovan, Thea Paneth, Edie Ravenelle, Anny Rey, Katie Pakos Rimer, Felicity Ryan, Ruth Schmidt, Ute Schmitt, Susan Shepherd, David Somers, Emma Westwater, Anne Wright, Lisa Yarger, and Marc Zegans.

Shellin' partner and sister from another mother, Barbara Atkinson, thank you.

Cynthia Anderson, Lynette Benton, Erica Ferencik, Margaret Muirhead, and Maureen Stanton, you are brilliant writers and generous friends who kept me laughing and paddling through the rough patches. I am deeply indebted to you.

Lisa Carey, you have been my writing shelter since our first day at Vermont College of Fine Arts. I finally get to thank you here.

Marilyn Osowiski and Diana Costello, if friendship is a treasure, you two are my city of gold.

Betsy Miller, thank you for shaking me upside down that day until the candy fireball came out of my throat. In addition to saving me over and over again, you've given me Robert, Kai, and Anja to make our family full and right.

Betty and Bill Miller, your spirits guided this book into being. Thank you for that and the gift of this lifetime.

To my students all over the world who regularly remind me that for writing to be rewarding, it must first be hard and humbling. In teaching all of you, I have learned so much.

Addie and Phinny—being your mother is more fun than pretty much anything I could ever do on this planet. Thank you for your unwavering faith in my dream and for making me so crazy proud of the people you are.

Mark, my one, my only. You never doubted or questioned this. You just kept holding up your torch of love to help light my path, and here we are. With all my heart, I thank you.

Sandra A. Miller's writing has appeared in more than one-hundred publications, including *The Christian Science Monitor,* *Spirituality & Health,* *Yankee,* *Family Fun,* and *The Boston Globe Magazine,* for which she is a regular correspondent. One of her essays was turned into a short film called "Wait," directed by Trudie Styler and starring Kerry Washington. She teaches writing at the University of Massachusetts, Lowell, and lives outside of Boston, Massachusetts, with her husband and two children.

Miller can be found at SandraAMiller.com, on Twitter @WriterSandraM, and on Instagram @sandra.a.miller.

BROWN PAPER PRESS

Brown Paper Press engages readers on topics of contemporary culture through quality writing and thoughtful design. Unbound by genre, our press delivers socially relevant works that advise, guide, inspire and amuse. We champion authors with new perspectives, strong voices, and original ideas that just might change the world.

For more information about new releases, author events, and special promotions, visit brownpaperpress.com.

215